Fraud Awareness

M. J. Veaudry

Front Cover

A collage of faces has been chosen for the front cover of this book because it uniquely depicts the character of fraud on the Internet. Unless you meet a person face-to-face, you really have no idea of who they are. Over the phone, you might be able to guess a person's gender and age, but very little else about them. On the Internet, all you know about a person is what they tell you. When you are emailing, chatting over social media or texting with someone, you really have no idea who they are. They could be one person or a group of people pretending to be one person. You really have no idea. You must never forget this simple fact.

Other Books by M. J. Veaudry

Fraud: Don't Be A Victim

Mike's Guide to Better Slot Play
Casino Games Demystified

Las Vegas Travel Tips
Ocean Cruise Travel Tips
Hawaii Travel Tips (coming soon)

2019 Edition

"4% of people are victims of almost 40% of frauds"
… Professor Ken Pease PhD, University of Manchester

Fraud Awareness is about a 21st century crime, personal fraud, that will affect every one of us. It is becoming so prevalent in our society that no one is immune to it. It is no longer a question of, if you will become a victim of one of these crimes, but when you will become a victim. What will you do when it happens?

The defining number for personal fraud is 37.5%. Police forces around the globe recognize this number as the percentage of people who when defrauded once, will be defrauded again.

This edition of the book will give the reader an incite into the business of fraud. How independent crews of criminals work collaboratively in a supply chain where our personal information is the underlying product. How crews buy this product, enhance it and then resell it, as it moves along the supply chain, until it can be used to perpetrate a fraud.

The book is designed to inform the reader about the major types of frauds that are prevalent today. How technology exacerbates an already bad situation. What you should be on the lookout for. What to do, to minimize any effect the fraud will have on you.

Understanding how these frauds work, is the best way to educate yourself. Learning what actions you need to take, before this happens, will mitigate your exposure and minimize your pain.

Mike

Copyright

By M. J. Veaudry

Dedication

This book is dedicated to everyone who is interested in learning more about fraud prevention and protection in today's complex, electronic world.

One of the biggest threats facing us today is the theft of our personal information and the subsequent use of this information against us.

Everyone is at risk. No one is immune from the damages that can be caused by such an attack. The best that we can do is to be aware of the dangers. Change our behavior, so we recognize when a threat is imminent. Take the necessary actions to minimize or eliminate the threat.

I would like to thank everyone who helped me with the content and how you clarified a number of the finer points for me.

I would like to thank everyone who attended my seminars on fraud over the last five years. Your excellent questions and suggestions have made the book much richer.

I would like to thank my wife who suffered through the writing, rewriting, proofreading, artwork and expletives along the way, this book could not have been written without her encouragement.

While I tried very hard to correct every possible error (grammar, spelling, punctuation, you name it), there are just so many times you can read the same material.

Any errors remaining are entirely my responsibility. If you find any, I apologize in advance. I hope you will forgive me.

M. J. Veaudry

Contents

1.0 Introduction

The fastest growing criminal activity in the world is FRAUD. There is no way of knowing exactly how big it is. No country or jurisdiction keeps consolidated records on frauds. There is not even a common agreement on how to categorize them or what to call them.

In Fraud Awareness we will examine personal frauds, not business frauds. We will start by taking a brief look at the history of personal fraud through the ages.

We will then examine the business of fraud to get a better understanding of who the fraudsters are and how they go about acquiring our personal information. The techniques they use, like phishing, pharming, vishing, spoofing and many others will be explained. We will follow the supply chain as our personal information is stolen, enriched and resold over the Dark Web. We will learn how criminals extract our personal information from the supply chain to perpetrate frauds against us.

Finally, we will try to make sense out of all these frauds we keep hearing about. We will group them into major types of frauds. We will examine each major type to identify what makes them unique. We will then use this information to identify some practical things that we can do to protect ourselves from them.

It is my hope that by analyzing personal frauds in this way and grouping the profusion of similar variations into major types we will be better able to deal with their complexities.

Personal fraud is not something new. It has been around for as long as people have collected wealth for themselves and their families. People have always coveted what other people have.

Let us start by talking a brief look at fraud through the ages.

2.0 A Short History of Fraud

Fraud is defined in the dictionary as a wrongful or criminal deception intended to result in financial or personal gain.

The phase, "fool me once, shame on you; fool me twice, shame on me" has been around a very long time. You can find it in many languages. This concept of being tricked by someone is nothing new. The oldest literary reference I could find for it was in the 1651 book by Anthony Weldon called The Court and Character of King James. However, some sources believe the phrase is much older.

In Roman mythology Fraus was the goddess of treachery. The Greek equivalent was Apate. In Celtic mythology, fraus was a very offensive curse word used to describe prostitutes. The Romans had a phrase, pia fraus used to describe deception. This is one of the earliest known phrases including the word fraud.

There are a number of references in the Bible to fraud. "That no man go beyond and defraud his brother in any matter: because that the Lord is the avenger of all such, as we also have forewarned you and testified." This quotation is from 1 Thessalonians 4:6.

Even older than this biblical quotation, there may be a reference in Homer's Iliad to fraud, dating back to eight hundred years before Christ. The text is very old and scholars can not agree on the exact wording, so it may or may not pertain to fraud.

The Middle Ages (from the fifth to the fifteenth century) was rampant with fraud. The most common frauds were related to food. Butchers would sell meat from animals that had died from illness. Bakers would bake with flour from moldy grain. Tavern owners would sell falsified beer made from mixtures of wild berries. These were all common practices in the Middle Ages.

Another major personal fraud was the certification of religious relics. Whenever an Abbott or a Bishop could get their hands on some bones, they would announce that the bones belonged to a saint. Pilgrims would flock to the church, to pray to the relic, pay for the privilege and hope to see a miracle.

With the arrival of the Renaissance (from the fifteenth to the seventeenth century) there was an explosion in the arts. As a result, many of the great works of art were forged in an attempt to swindle buyers by offering these forgeries as the real thing.

Some of the best forgers of this Age were the great artists themselves. Michelangelo perpetrated one of the most notorious frauds in the Renaissance. In 1496, when just a youth, he forged a sculpture of the sleeping cupid, based on a drawing from the ancient Greeks. He then buried it in acidic earth to give it an appearance of great age.

The plan was to pass it off as an antiquity so it would fetch a higher price. The piece was sold through a dealer, Baldassare del Milanese to Cardinal Raffaello Riario of San Giorgio. The Cardinal eventually found out that the sculpture was a forgery and demanded his money back from the dealer.

Michelangelo was allowed to keep his share of the profit, since the Cardinal was not upset with the youth, only the dealer. The forgery was lost in the seventeenth century. If it is ever found, it would command an enormous sum today, as an original Michelangelo fake.

It was not until the early seventeen century that frauds emerged in America. Shortly after the Pilgrims arrived, snake oil ploys started to circulate as a cure for almost everything. These scams have been around for hundreds of years. They have migrated into the cancer miracle cures and internet health cures we see today.

The other big fraud in early America was land fraud. As the original thirteen colonies were established, men who had been given grants from the English Crown owned the land. These men in turn resold the land off to individuals. Although many of the early land dealings were legitimate, it didn't take long for land swindlers to emerge.

The usual victims of these land frauds were new immigrants. As settlers moved west, vast tracts of land became available through government acquisitions. Legislators and bureaucrats found new opportunities to accept bribes and collude with land swindlers. Legal protection of deeds, claims and land records came into existence to discourage, but certainly not eliminate, land and mineral swindles.

Even today, land fraud continues to be one of the major opportunities for fraud and deception. If you don't believe me, I know someone who has some great swampland for sale in Florida.

Fraud continues to roll across American history like waves onto a beach. Fraud rises and falls with innovations and ultimate corrections. The most important thing we should learn from this brief history, is that the incidents of fraud are most prolific when they are associated with those things most coveted by society.

Whether this was the hope people sought in the Middle Ages. The confirmation they received when they prayed to the Church's relics. Or the land people later coveted, upon which to build a better life.

Fraud has always followed society's major aspirations. Today it is no different. As society strives for wealth and financial independence or health and longevity, fraud is close behind. With the temptation to exploit society's vulnerabilities, using the latest technology to accomplish its objective, fraud is always there, lurking in the background, waiting to claim its next, unsuspecting victim.

3.0 The Business of Fraud

Gone are the days where the individual confidence man would try to fleece a mark. Today organized crime is involved on a big scale. In 2009 is was estimated that almost 70% of all frauds worldwide were linked to organized crime. In 2016 this number had risen to 80%. In 2018, it is estimated that 90% of all mass-marketing frauds are carried out by organized crime.

The days of back rooms filled with money counting machines, bookies taking bets and laying off odds and people running the numbers on every street corner are long gone. These have now been replaced with "boiler rooms" where people sit at computers and hack into retail and financial computer systems, work the phones and crank out counterfeit credit cards on a massive scale.

Is this profitable? Absolutely. According to The Financial Cost of Fraud 2018 report, by Crowe Clark Whitehill, together with the University of Portsmouth's Centre for Counter Fraud Studies, the annual cost of fraud is almost $4 trillion dollars. This number includes both business and personal frauds. There is no definitive split between the two.

If we make a very conservative assumption that personal fraud is only 5% of this worldwide number or $200 billion. We know from experience that only 15% of the population, on average, report a personal fraud and only 5% of seniors report a personal fraud. This means that the actual value of personal fraud worldwide could easily exceed $1 trillion.

The other thing you need to know about the business of fraud is that it has a very low operating cost. Unlike other companies, fraudsters do not need a place to work. A typical office might be a local Starbucks with free internet service. It could be a vacant warehouse with phone services and an internet connection. These people are not salaried employees, they do not get vacation pay or need health insurance. They work irregular hours and they only get paid when they are successful at delivering results.

If personal fraud was a single business entity, it would be the largest company in the world. With a market capitalization well in excess of one trillion dollars.

So what does this mean to the individual? What does this mean to you? It means that personal frauds are going to be with us for a very long time.

One trend that we can all see occurring is an increase in the frequency of personal fraud attacks. Just think of the number of phone calls and emails you are now getting compared to just a few years ago.

Fraud attacks that once were confined to a geographic area, a city, a state or a country, have now gone global as a result of the Internet. Criminals can now target individuals in other countries because of the ubiquity and anonymity of the Internet. A person receiving an email has no idea who the sender is or where they are located. This is one of the major reasons that the number of personal frauds are increasing rapidly.

Before leaving this chapter, I would like to talk briefly about how the business of fraud is organized. Most of us are familiar with the typical hierarchical nature of a large organization, like the one shown here. There is a Board of Directors, a CEO, numerous levels of executives, middle and lower level managers and of course the staff, usually organized into departments designed to produce products that are then delivered to customers. These organizations have a lot of infrastructure, processes and procedures to keep the company going. Their overhead can also be very expensive.

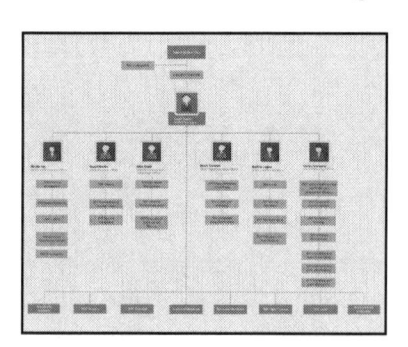

Unlike a large multinational corporation the business of fraud is structured more like a horizontal supply chain of relatively small groups or crews of people who interact with each other through the Dark Web. These criminals buy data from crews in the supply chain, add value to this data and then resell it to other crews in the supply chain. Every time this happens, the crew selling the data is making a profit. Eventually, the data will be bought by a crew that has the knowledge and expertise to convert the data into cash. This usually occurs when a fraud is perpetrated.

Because there is no honor among thieves, most of the supply chain transactions take place on the Dark Web. This allows each crew in the supply chain to remain anonymous and ensures a secure payment method that can not be traced back to the crews involved.

Fraud is a cash business. Crews in the supply chain that make a profit will survive, crews that do not, will disappear and be replaced by others. This is a very effective organization structure for the business of fraud.

Some typical crews in the supply chain.
So what are these crews doing? That depends directly on their skills and experience. Here are just a few examples of fictional crews in the supply chain and what they might be doing.

Oleg is 28 years old. He has a Masters Degree in computational mathematics and cybernetics from Lomonosov Moscow State University. He works for a small analytics company in Moscow that is funded by the government. He works with five other young people out of a small apartment located on Kutuzovsky Prospekt. They are engaged in hacking into foreign financial and government computer systems to steal personal data from customers and citizens. The crew is managed by Major Vasiliev of the GRU.

Faruq is 24 years old. He lives in Kaduna, Nigeria a city of just over a million people. He works with a crew of five other people who are running romance scams on women in the West. The crew is set up in Hamald's Cyber Cafe in Market Road where the free Wi-Fi is very good. They run two twelve hour shifts so they can chat with the women whenever it is necessary. All chat sessions are recorded for continuity, since anyone of the six could pick up the chat if needed. When they are not chatting, they troll social media and dating sites looking for new targets.

Vinnie is 45 years old. He lives in New York's Lower East Side. He has lived in this neighbourhood his entire life. He has a small store front on Orchard Street where he runs a used book store. His real business however is in the basement. He has several high-end plastic card printers, embossing machine, portable card readers and laptop computers, capable of turning out over 10,000 counterfeit credit cards a day. He employees six people in his crew who run the counterfeiting operation and do double duty in the book store. Vinnie offers a custom service where he will include fake drivers' licenses synchronized with the names on the stolen credit cards, when his customers provide photo id for the driver's license. The book store is a good front for Vinnie's operation, as he is always moving boxes of stuff in and out of the store.

Robert is 18 years old. He is a high school senior at Palo Verde High School in Summerlin, a suburban community on the western side of Las Vegas. He works the busier parts of the Strip and Fremont St. His boss, Chuck provides him with a high-end portable skimmer that fits in his backpack. He hustles through these busy tourist areas collecting the data stored on their smart cards as he goes. No one notices him and it is easy to push your way through a large crowd, especially when you are a teenager. Robert has been doing this for a few years now to make pocket money. When the skimmer beeps that it is full, he returns it to Chuck who downloads the data to a computer, before handing it back to Robert to try another area.

All of the crews in the supply chain are performing one of four basic functions. They are either stealing raw data to feed the supply chain, phishing and pharming the data to add value to it or converting the enhanced data into cash by perpetrating a fraud.

This book is focused mostly on the last step in this process and the frauds that are perpetrated on us. We will discuss in some detail the various types of frauds that are common and how to protect ourselves from becoming a victim. However, in order to better understand these frauds, we will take a look at how organized crime goes about acquiring the data that will be used against us. To the extent that we can prevent criminals from acquiring this data in the first place, we may be able to reduce the number and severity of these crimes.

Let's start at the beginning of the supply chain and the crews that steal the raw data in the first place.

3.1 Theft

Criminals have many ways to steal data. Most of the data that is stolen has nothing to do with Identity Theft. I know that the media likes to call any theft of our data, Identity Theft. It makes for good headlines but the reality is, that in most cases, the thief could care less about who the person is whose information is stolen. They are just stealing data, the identity of the person is not important to them. So how do these crews go about stealing our data.

3.1.1 Computer Hacking

The cheapest way for criminals to steal data is by hacking into

 computer systems that store lots of raw data. The harder it is to break into a system, the more valuable the data and the more it will be worth when it is resold.

Depending on where the computer hackers steal the raw data, they may also have access to the individual's email address, home address, phone number as well as other personal data. The more data they have, the more valuable the information.

The unit price is usually quite small, often only a few cents. Although by volume it could amount to a large amount of money, even in the millions of dollars. These people are hardly ever caught and because they often work off-shore it is almost impossible for law enforcement to lay their hands on them.

In 2016 there were 4,149 confirmed data breeches worldwide with over 4.2 billion records stolen. More than 3.2 billion records than were stolen in 2013, the previous all-time high.

Let us fast forward to 2018. At least 87 million records and probably more were breached on Facebook. Who can forget how a political data firm called Cambridge Analytica collected the personal information of 50 million Facebook users via an app that scraped details about people's personalities, social networks, and activity on the platform. Despite Cambridge Analytica's claim that it only had information on 30 million users, Facebook determined the original estimate was in fact low. In April, the company notified 87 million members on its platform that their data had been shared. The important thing to note about this breach, is that credit card information was not the target.

On June 4, 2018 a security researcher reached out to the Chief Information Security Officer of online genealogy platform MyHeritage and revealed they had found a file labeled "myheritage" on a private server outside the company. Upon inspection of the file, officials at MyHeritage determined that the file contained the email addresses of all users who had signed up with MyHeritage prior to October 26, 2017.

According to a statement published by the company, the file also contained their hashed passwords but not payment information. MyHeritage was relying on third-party service providers to process members' payments. Because the service also stores family tree and DNA data on servers separate from those that store email addresses, MyHeritage said there was no reason to believe that, that information had been exposed or compromised.

In September 2018 a major computer breach of 1.1 billion records was discovered at AADHAAR (Hindi word meaning foundation). India has one of the most advanced biometric identification systems in the world. Each citizen is assigned a 12-digit unique identity number, based on their biometric and demographic data. This information is used for all services provided by the government.

Reporters with the Tribune News Service paid 500 rupees (about $7.00 US) for login credentials to a service being offered by anonymous sellers over WhatsApp. Using the service, the reporters could enter any Aadhaar number to retrieve data on the queried citizen, including name, address, photo, phone number and email address. An additional payment of 300 rupees gave access to software through which anyone could print an ID card for any citizen. The data breach is believed to have compromised the personal information of all 1.1 billion citizens registered in India.

3.1.2 Skimming

Skimmers do not have the computer skills that hackers have, so they rely on low-tech tools to steal data.

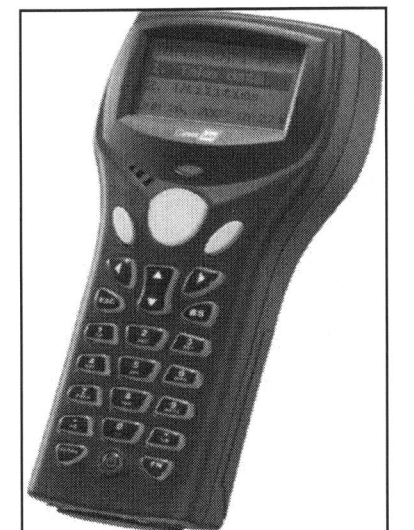

Portable skimming devices, like the one shown here, can read personal data from unprotected smart cards by just being close to them.

You can buy a top of the line skimming device on the Internet for less than a thousand dollars. They are the size of a TV remote control device and easily fit into a pocket or a back pack.

All the criminal has to do is walk through a crowd with the skimming device turned on to collect the data on the magnetic stripe from any unprotected cards that it comes into contact with. This data is lower quality compared to what a computer hacker might be able to get, but it is still valuable to criminals who have the resources to produce counterfeit credit cards that can be used to convert purchases into cash.

A smart card is any card that transmits an RFID (radio frequency identification) signal to a card reader. A typical smart card will have

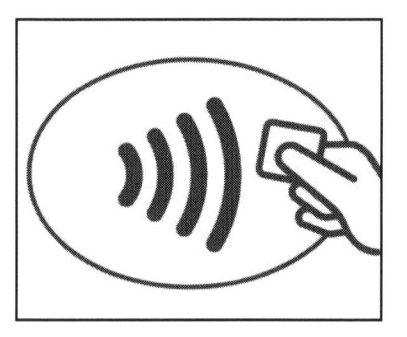

a symbol like this on it. These smart cards will allow customers to use a tap capability to make a purchase. These cards are popular with millennials.

The criminal does not have to buy an expensive card reader, like the skimmer shown above. A very cheap card reader like the one shown here costs less than $100. All the criminal has to do is scan your credit card to capture all of the information stored on the magnetic stripe.

A card reader this size can hold up to 3,000 credit cards. The

reader also comes with a USB cable that can be attached to a computer to download the data captured on the reader. Some readers can even connect wirelessly to a computer or smart phone.

These devises are so small and light that a criminal can attach a velcro strip to them and wear it on their person. This is a common way for a waitress, who drops your credit card on the floor when paying your bill, and while reaching to pick it up, scans the card (attached to a velcro strip fastened to her thigh) before returning it to you. When she picks the card up she also makes note of the cvv number on the card.

If you go through a drive-through to make a purchase. The clerk smiles at you, takes your card and in one smooth motion, swipes your card twice. Once on their own card reader and once for the store. This is all done while making note of the cvv number on the card without you even noticing.

Gas pump skimmers are also popular among criminals and are much harder to detect. They can be easily hidden inside a gas pump and when a customer's debit or credit card is tapped or swiped, they will read all of the data on the card, including the PIN if it is used. All the crew has to do is pay a gas station employee to look the other way, usually late at night, while they use the employee's key to open the pump and install the skimmer. These skimmers are wireless devices, so all the criminal has to do is drive up to the pump once a week, fill up with gas while his buddy is sitting in the car and downloading the data from the pump onto his laptop.

Gas stations that know they have problems with these criminals now ask customers to pay inside if they are using a debit card. This is one way they can protect you and limit your bank's liability.

3.1.3 Tampering

Tampering is another method frequently used by criminals to steal

 payment card details from banking machines and PIN card readers. It literally takes less than twenty seconds for a professional to swap out a merchant's PIN card reader, like this one and replace it with a fraudulent machine that will steal the customer's payment card data while still processing the transaction.

To help merchants detect these fraudulent readers, law enforcement will encourage retailers to put distinctive markings on their machines. Another way you might identify a fraudulent reader is if your payment card slides too far into the machine. This might

be an indicator that the machine has been tampered with. Some criminals use a fake overlay that just snaps over the original card reader.

If criminals are tampering with bank machines they may not only have the individual's debit card information, but they might also have their PIN. This would make the card data very valuable.

This picture shows a faux front for an ATM machine that was seized on a police raid at a factory in Taiwan, where they were being manufactured. This is by far the most deceptive way to tamper with

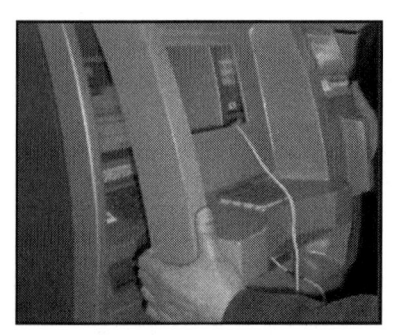 a bank machine. It does mot take very long to install one of these faux fronts but we hardly ever see them on banking machines that are in a bank branch. These are found on private label machines installed in remote locations where it is unlikely to find surveillance equipment.

What can be found on any banking machine, even those that are in the lobby of a bank branch, are tools like a hidden camera over the PIN pad, a cash trap placed over the cash dispenser, a Lebanese loop to block a debit card from being read by the machine, a false front placed over the card reader slot and even a PIN overlay (a thin transparent cover placed over the keypad) to record and transmit the PIN you just entered, with a date and time stamp.

3.1.4 Protecting Yourself from Theft

So how do we protect ourselves from criminals who want to steal our data?

The simple answer is that there is very little we can do to protect ourselves from computer hackers. These criminals are almost never identified and if they are, they are probably working off-shore. This makes it almost impossible for law enforcement to arrest them. Even if they were arrested, it would probably be too late to retrieve the stolen data that has almost certainly been sold on the Dark Web. We are relying heavily on the governments and organizations who have our personal data to protect it for us. Did I really say this?

Nevertheless, there are things that we can do to protect the data that is in our possession. It is only prudent to do so. While this will offer us little protection against computer hackers, this is not the case with criminals who are skimming and tampering. Here are some suggestions to reduce your risk of having your personal data stolen.

- This is not one we talked about previously but it is pet peeve of mine. We all have to learn to minimize the amount of personal data we carry with us. Only carry what you need. If you are a woman, stop carrying a purse. No one needs to carry their social security card, a check book, extra credit cards, personal papers anything that, if stolen, could compromise you.

- Place your smart cards into an RFID wallet or protective sleeve.

- Cover the cvv number on the front or back of all smart cards with a small dot (you can buy a sheet of these at any Dollar Store) or use a piece of green painter's tape. The dots are harder to remove, so it is easy to see if they have been tampered with. If you do need to take the dot off, you can put it back on until you replace it with another dot. Whatever you use to cover the cvv number needs to be thin enough to allow the card to slide through a PIN card reader.

- Always go with your card. Never hand it off to someone else to process. I know, this may be difficult in an upscale restaurant where the waiter wants to take your card away to process it. Just be polite and offer to go with them.

- Alway put your card into the PIN reader yourself. If the card reader is behind the merchant and not out front where you can use it, do not make the purchase or refuse to pay unless you can put the card into the machine yourself. There may be nothing wrong, but you never know.

- When you go to a gas station, try to avoid the pumps furthest from the attendant's both. Criminals who install gas pump skimmers prefer to do so in the pumps furthest from the attendant. This makes it easier for them to download the data from the skimmer to their laptop without being seen by the attendant.

Criminals who tamper with devices are usually very good at what they do. It is often very difficult to even tell if a device has been tampered with. Here are a few guidelines you can follow when faced with using a PIN device or a banking machine, that might make the transaction more secure for you.

- When you put the card into the PIN reader watch how far the card goes into the reader. If the reader has been tampered with, the card will need to go deeper into the machine to traverse the extra electronics that have been added to capture the data on the card twice, once for the merchant and once for the criminal. Make a habit out of noticing how deep your card usually goes into the reader, so you will recognize it when it goes in further. Without getting too technical, you should be able to see at least 1 inch on the left and right edge of your card. Because of the shape of the card reader, it will be less than an inch in the middle of the card, about 13/16th of an inch.

- Do not use an ATM that is not in a bank lobby. There are over 400,000 ATMs installed in the country. Over half of these are owned by independent operators. It is estimated that 5% (over 10,000) machines are operated by organized crime. It is easier for criminal to tamper with these machines.

- Learn to fully cover your PIN as it is being entered. By fully covering it, I mean place your hand or a wallet completely over the keypad, slide your other hand under the top hand and enter your PIN. If you get it wrong, do it again. It will take a little practice. Do not tell anyone your PIN.

- Never use a keypad at a banking machine that is covered with anything. If it has a thin plastic overlay over the keypad, go to another machine and tell the branch about it.

- If you are worried about the machine at all, give it the wiggle test. That's right, the wiggle test. Place you hand firmly on the card reader, cash draw and keypad and try to move them. If they wiggle at all, leave the machine and tell the branch about it. Look above the keypad for any hidden cameras.

- If you are a senior or elderly person or you know someone who is, encourage them to go into the branch and use the teller, not the ATM. There are criminals who lurk in the lobbies and try to help older people who seem to be having a problem with the machine. Trust me, they are not there to help you.

So what do these criminals do with the data they have stolen. A few of them, if they have collected enough data to perpetrate a crime, will do so.

For example, a crew using a Lebanese loop in a banking machine to capture a bank card when it is entered into the card reader, will have one of their crew in the lobby to watch when the victim enters their PIN and the machine tells them it is not valid. Unknown to them, is the fact that the loop has not only trapped their card in the machine, but has also covered the chip, making it impossible for the card to verify what they have entered.

The fraudster will then approach them to see if they can help. They will watch the victim enter their PIN again and will explain that the same thing has happened to them. They will offer to watch the machine while the victim goes inside the branch at get help. As soon as the victim enters the branch, the fraudster will use a small tool designed to snag the loop and remove it and the card from the machine. This only takes a few seconds and they are gone. When the victim returns with help, there is nothing left to show them. The criminal and their card has disappeared. The fraudster has gone to another branch. Armed with the card and the PIN, they are emptying the victim's bank account.

Most of the crews that have been stealing our data will be selling it on the Dark Web to other crews in the supply chain who will add value to it before reselling it.

Short of stealing our raw data, there are only two ways that a crew can add value to what has been stolen. They can phish (pronounced fish) for it or they can pharm (pronounced farm) for it.

3.2 Phishing and Pharming

Phishing and pharming are twenty-first century words for twenty-first century cybercrime.

Phishing is a concatenation of two words, phony and fishing. It describes a criminal's effort to trick a target into disclosing personal information.

Pharming is a concatenation of two words, phony and farming. It describes a criminal's effort to trick a target into visiting a fraudulent website by clicking on a concealed hyperlink, usually in an email.

The other way fraudsters trick people into visiting fraudulent websites is by setting up websites that purport to have information that could be legitimately linked to an unassuming search. No one ever calls their fraudulent website, SoftwareAttack.com, instead they might call it Malware101.com. The latter site would probably turn up on any search looking for information on malware.

Phishing and pharming are usually attempted over email or on the Internet because these venues are ubiquitous and very inexpensive. A variation of phishing that is done over the phone is called vishing. It is also very effective in reaching a large number of people even though it is more expensive than email or the Internet.

Social media is also a prime location on the Internet for criminals to collect personal information and download malware without the target's knowledge.

We will examine phishing and pharming in three venues; social media, email and the Internet. We will also look at some practical things we can do to protect ourselves from this type of cybercrime.

3.2.1 Over Social Media

One way fraudsters go about getting personal information on a target is to follow them on social media. In the US, as of the third quarter of 2018, there were 214 million Facebook users, 67 million Twitter users, 150 million LinkedIn users and 105 million Instagram users. This is a rich pool from which to get personal information on almost anyone in the country.

Also, do not make the mistake that these sites are secure. Remember the story of Cambridge Analytica and the Facebook hack during the 2016 election. Facebook users might think that they are making their pages private by only making them available to their 'friends'. However, when you become 'friends' with someone on Facebook, three things happen.

- You appear on your friend's friend list.
- You appear on their profile page.
- With the click of a mouse, someone can hop from your friend's profile to yours. There is no privacy protocol to stop them. Now think about how many people you know that are on Facebook and 'friend' people they do not know.

The simpler option the fraudster has, of course, is to just follow the target on Facebook.

Fraudsters like to search these sites for information on particular individuals that they are targeting. While it can be time-consuming to search Facebook, there is a browser search that makes it easy, www.Facebook.com inurl:<name you are looking for>. If the fraudster is looking for a particular person's Facebook page all they have to do is replace "<name you are looking for>" with the person's name and it will pop up immediately.

UVRX (www.uvrx.com/social) is a collection of Google custom searches put together for Facebook, Twitter, LinkedIn, Youtube, Google Plus, Instagram, Myspace and other popular sites that will quickly search for a person, if they are on one of these sites.

These are just a few of the free social media search engines available to help fraudsters track people on social media. Fraudsters have access to many other tools that make it easy for them to find people on the Internet. If you are on social media, it is almost impossible to hide.

Here are just a few of the scams that are common on social media sites.

See who's viewed your profile. This scam takes advantage of the curiosity of Facebook users and might pop up as an ad while you are browsing the site. You will be prompted to download an app with the promise of being able to see who has viewed your profile. The thing is, Facebook does not actually give this information out, even to third-party applications. All you are actually doing is handing over access to your Facebook account, including your personal details and possibly banking information. This is also common practice on LinkedIn.

A Facebook 'dislike' button is something users have been longing for, for some time. Scammers capitalize on this, by posting ads for such a feature. These ads lead to pages that look like they are run by Facebook, but that actually include links to phishing sites asking for personal information.

Clickbait is defined as web content that is aimed at generating online advertising revenue, especially at the expense of quality or accuracy, relying on sensationalist headlines to attract click-throughs and to encourage forwarding of the material over online social networks. Once you click-through, you are prompted to enter your Facebook credentials to view the article, thus giving criminals full access to your account.

Fake celebrity news scams involve a clickbait headline on Facebook relaying some fake celebrity news, such as the death of a well-known star, or a new relationship in Hollywood. Once you click, you are prompted to enter your Facebook credentials to view the article, thus giving criminals full access to your account.

Impersonation scams are based on how easy it is to create a social media account. There is nothing stopping someone from creating an exact replica of your public profile. They can then reach out to your friends and family with 'friend' or 'follow' requests and once connected, pose as you. These trusted connections can then be used for a whole host of purposes, such as spreading malware or requesting money for made-up scenarios.

'Likes'/'follows' scam. With many users across social platforms desperate for 'likes' and 'follows,' scammers have capitalized by offering just that. One app released in 2013 called InstLike asked for usernames and passwords in return for 'likes' and 'follows'. In fact, they simply collected the credentials of 100,000 users and turned them into participants in a large social botnet. Basically, the app did deliver on its promise but used the accounts of those who signed up to do so. What's more, within the app, people were encouraged to pay fees for additional 'follows' and 'likes'.

3.2.2 Over eMail
The other common way to go phishing is over email. Everyone's email address has been stolen and you can purchase stolen email addresses on the Internet for next to nothing. However, having an email address does not mean that your message to a target will get through to them.

All email applications today have excellent spam filters, so it is likely that any email fraudsters send to someone on their stolen email list, will probably end up in that person's trash can.

But wait, fraudsters already know this. Well at least the good ones do. They also have a way to get around this. It's called spoofing. They accomplish this by the forgery of an email header so that the message appears to have originated from someone or somewhere that the target recognizes. It works for the fraudster because email was never designed to ensure that senders were who they said they were.

The example here appears to be from Cineplex Odeon. It is designed to get my attention and it did. The English and the graphics are good. It claims that there have been a number of unsuccessful attempts to login to my account and my account has been locked. The box at the bottom 'Reset Password' is a hyperlink. If I were to click on this it would take me to a fraudulent website where it will ask for my card's expiry date and cvv number. I can assume that they already have my card number and cardholder name. That is a good touch. It should make me feel confident that this request is legitimate.

This is actually a pretty good phishing email. I know this because I did not press the hyperlink. Instead, I signed into Netflix using the official website and checked my account information directly. My card had not expired and my account was still active.

A lot of phishing emails are just bulk emails that get sent out to everyone, think of them like the flyers that we still get in our surface mail. Whether you are a customer of the company in the banner or not, it does not matter, you get the email anyway. Just like you get the flyer.

Forging an email about telephone charges as being sent from AT&T or Verizon is also pretty good, since they both have more customers than other service providers. People who are not customers of Verizon or AT&T will just delete the email message.

This kind of spoofing is just a numbers game. The fraudster does not care if the target is a customer of the company on the header. They will reach enough people who are customers, to make it worth their while.

Fraudsters that are more sophisticated might actually send phishing emails from you, to contacts in your address book. This use to be done with viruses that would invade your computer and access your email program. The virus would then start sending out the emails using your address book. While that is still possible, it does not happen very often anymore. Most email programs now protect against unauthorized address book access. What is more likely, is that your email account has been compromised.

There are a number of ways this could happen. Having a weak password that is easy to guess, your account credentials being sniffed at an open Wi-Fi hotspot, using your email on a shared computer or having your account credentials stolen from your service provider without your knowledge.

These are just some of the ways that fraudsters try to hook you when phishing over email. The more dangerous thing that happens over email however, is pharming.

Fraudsters who are pharming just want you to click on something in the message that will link you to a fraudulent website from where they will download malware onto your device. Malware is defined as any software that is intended to damage or disable your device.

Most computers today have some kind of virus protection. After all, viruses have been around for a long time. Frederick Cohen coined the phrase in 1983. Even so, it is estimated that 24% of home computers still do not have antivirus software installed.

Malware is a class of software that is used to describe all sorts of unwanted or malicious code. For our purpose, we will focus on four major classes of malware that are common today.

Trojan programs conceal malicious code within a seemingly useful application. These are often found in free software on the Internet. It might even be shared with others or downloaded from seemingly legitimate websites. The game, utility, or whatever you have downloaded, typically performs as you would expect. However, it can be very damaging for the unsuspecting victim. Trojans have been known to inject fake transactions to drain the victims bank accounts. They might just steal your personal information to sell it on the Dark Web. This malware is very dangerous.

Worms are similar to viruses in the way they work, but they do not require the user to launch an infected program to activate them. A worm can copy itself and move from computer to computer by attaching itself to an email or text message you might innocently send to a friend. This enables the worm to move undetected from computer to computer. Internet worms are dangerous and they can be very difficult to remove.

Spyware refers to software that spies on your computer and steals passwords or other personal information. If you have a webcam attached to your computer, spyware can peek though your webcam. Smartphones have become a target for spyware. It can be used to track texts, chats, call history, photos, GPS and much more while being almost undetectable.

Viruses run when a user launches an infected program or boots from an infected disk or USB drive. Viruses keep a low profile and spread quietly though an infected system. Most viruses are mindlessly destructive. These are the least dangerous form of malware.

It is very difficult to monetize a virus. Criminals have fixed this problem by developing malware like the types identified above. This is not an exhaustive list by any means and new malware is being developed every day. It was estimated that in 2014 there were 317 million new pieces of malware released. Nearly 1 million threats a day. In the first half of 2018, G Data Security, estimates the number on new malware threats to be over 2.3 billion. On an annual basis, this is a thousand times more than we saw just four years ago.

The terms antivirus and anti-malware are becoming blurred. Most security companies now refer to antivirus software as protection against malware. It is always a good idea to check with them before you buy, to make sure you understand what malware the product is protecting against.

3.2.3 Over the Internet

The Internet is a dangerous place. According to Netcraft, an internet services company based in Bath, England, there were 1.8 billion websites on the Internet in January, 2018. Most of these websites get almost no visitors.

This may sound like a big number but this is only the part of the Internet that we see with our commercial browsers. According to one Dutch researcher, there are at least 4.5 billion websites that have been indexed by search engines and this is only a fraction of what is really out there. Some researchers believe there are 300 - 500 new websites created on the Internet every minute.

Fraudsters mainly use the Internet for pharming. They are constantly adding new websites and dropping off old ones. The main intention is to get you to visit their website under some pretence. It might be a free software tool that will enhance your computer. It might be a game. Malware authors frequently hide their malware in software promoted as cracked versions of popular internet games. Games for children are also becoming popular targets to hide malware.

What we do know for sure is that most malware attacks are now launched from the Internet and not from executable files (found in email). Here are just a few of the scams on the Internet where malware might be lurking.

The free Wi-Fi scam is used by criminals who set up a free Wi-Fi hotspot that does not require a password. Once you are connected, the scammer can access virtually any information you send over the Internet. If you log into your bank or check your credit card balance online, the scammer can get your username and password. If you place a mobile order, the scammer can get all your credit card and personal information. They can sometimes even access information in your browser history or decrypt information sent through secure websites.

Malware masquerading in gaming software has become a very popular way for fraudsters to promote their products. In September, 2017 a new strain of malware called ExpensiveWall was found lurking in about 50 apps in the Google Play store. It had been downloaded between 1 million and 4.2 million times. Even after Google removed the offending software, a new version of the malware appeared in Google Play. The same situation has also occurred in the Apple App store.

Online shopping scams are becoming very popular. A lot of people shop online today. Why not. It is easy, fun and there are some great deals, not to mention free delivery. Take Amazon and Wayfair as just two good examples. But watch out for websites that are not legitimate. There are a bunch of scammers who will feature beautiful clothes on their website, but when you purchase anything, you will not get it. Some of them might lure you in with offering hard to get brands or inexpensive knock-offs.

General information scams are hidden in websites that do nothing more than download malware to your device. All they do is register a good sounding website name with plenty of keywords that can be picked up by your web browser. When you are using the Internet for research on some topic that might interest you, you find a link to this bogus site and as soon as you click on it, it starts to download malware to your machine. Some sites do not even try to hide it. You might see it as an endless stream of executable files being loaded onto your computer. The site might actually have no content at all, just the download.

Sponsored stories and you may like links that you often find when browsing the web are not always safe to go to. These links could take you to a fraudulent website where malware can be downloaded to your device. Every time you see one of these links make sure that they specify the sponsor. If there is no sponsor, do not click on it. If there is a sponsor identified, then do a search on that name before you click on it. Find out if the sponsor is legitimate.

Avoid known traps on the Internet. There are certain sites that are know to be risky and you should not go to them. Avoid pornographic sites, they are well-known sources of malware. Downloading images can definitely get you infected. Ads on any of these sites can be compromised. Avoid using Adobe Flash, it is a security nightmare. Avoid using Java as a web plug-in. If you need a web plug-in use HTML5 instead. You need to be increasingly vigilant about what you add to your browser. You might think that these plug-ins are all about helping you, but you could be wrong.

3.2.4 Protecting Yourself From Phishing and Pharming

So how can we protect ourselves on social media, email or the Internet from phishing and pharming scams? Here are some of the actions you should consider taking immediately.

Social Media is going to be the most difficult place to protect yourself from fraudsters. These platforms are not mature and the security features are weak. The best advice I can give you is do not use them. I know, you are already on them or there is a lot of pressure to be on them, so what do you do now.

The first thing to remember is that there is no privacy on the Internet. It is impossible to permanently delete anything from the Internet. Somewhere on the Internet, someone is backing-up something at sometime. Do not put anything on the Internet that you do not want the whole world to see.

This does not mean that we should not use social media sites, just that we should be very, very careful about how we use them and what we post on them. Here are some practical things you can do to protect yourself on social media.

- Consider starting over with a new account. Delete or deactivate your old account. Use a pseudonym when you set up your new profile. Use a fake address and phone number as well. Consider masking all of your personal information, age, birthdate, marital status, education and so on. This does not prevent you from telling your family, relatives and close personal friends what you have done. It also does not prevent you from sharing information with them. It actually might be more fun doing this. It will make it harder for unwanted eyes to make you a target.

- Create a different and strong password for each social media account. A strong password will have at least 12 characters consisting of letters (upper and lower case), numbers and special characters. Do not use words or phrases. Do not use repeating numbers or letters.

- Carefully check the social media's privacy settings and use the highest level security available on the site.

- Never allow automatic logins. Do not let your browser remember your login and password. Do not store your passwords on your smart phone.

- If you have the Flashlight app on your computer or smart phone, delete it immediately. Hackers can use it to take personal information, contacts, the phone's video camera and GPS.

- Turn off geotagging (GPS or location-based services) on your smart phone. If you post a picture on your social media site when geotagging is turned on, anyone viewing this picture can identify exactly where it was take.

The last thing I want you to think about is removing all third-party Facebook plug-ins. Some sites you visit will require you to login using Facebook. When you do, they will ask you to 'trust them'.

This is very risky. Third-party logins are mini applications that monitor your behavior and grab information about your habits. This is what Facebook and Google use to push content to you that you might be interested in.

I do not expect you to be able or willing to take all of these precautions when you use social media. Whatever you can do, will help protect yourself and it is better than doing nothing.

Email is used by everyone who has a computer. It is one of the most ubiquitous platforms that we have at our disposal. It is also a mature platform. It has been around for a long time and email systems are relatively rich in functionality and security features.

Here are some practical things that you can do to protect yourself on email from phishing and harming scams.

- Check your mail system preferences and look at security settings. Do not automatically open attachments. Turn this feature off. This will prevent you from automatically downloading a malware attachment to your device without first deciding wether you want to open the attachment.

- Change your security settings to turn off automatically loading remote content. This is important because even a picture can hide a link to a fraudulent site that could download malware to your device. After you open the message and verify that is it legitimate, you can then click on load remote content and view the images. This is similar to, but not exactly the same, as opening an attachment.

- Set your junk mail filters as strong as possible. Make sure you send the junk mail to a junk mail box, not your inbox. You do not want to open this mail by mistake. Learn to delete junk mail without opening it.

- Clean out your address book. Get ride of all the old entries. I know, it's nice to keep the names of everyone you ever met. But this is also a way for fraudsters to trick you into thinking that someone you use to know is sending you a legitimate message.

- Learn to do a mouse over. Before you open any hyperlink in an email, run your mouse over the link without clicking on it. When you set the mouse on the link, without clicking it, a window will open up showing you where the link is pointed. If the link does not point to where you think it should, do not click on it.

- If the email purports to come from a trusted source and they want you to click on something to go to their site, do not do this. Do an internet search yourself to find the site. Then checkout what they are asking you to do.

- Backup your device regularly. Install all updates to your operating system and applications as soon as you get them.

- Use a strong password to lock your device. If you have any biometric security features you might also want to use them. If you have a feature to destroy all of the data on your device (smart phone for example) after a certain number of failed attempts to breech your device's security, turn it on.

The Internet is where most of the pharming frauds are found. Fraudsters phish using a combination of email and fraudulent websites. We are seeing a lot more fraudulent websites springing up to hook people who are surfing the Internet and unwillingly get snagged by them. Much of this can be attributed to the tools that exist to build, in relatively short order, a good quality website. The poorly designed websites with bad graphics and broken English, that were incomprehensible to understand, are a thing of the past. Today's fraudulent websites look every bit as good as any corporation could produce. So be wary when your internet surfing takes you to one of these sites.

Here are just a few practical things you can do to prevent falling prey to one of these websites.

- Do not use public open Wi-Fi. If you have to use free Wi-Fi consider installing a VPN (virtual private network) on your device for these occasions. The VPN will encrypt whatever you send over the Internet and keep your communication secure. According to itportal.com the five best VPN products for 2018 are: ExpressVPN, IPVanish, VyprVPN, NordVPN and TunnelBear, in that order.

- Instal a good quality antivirus product on your device that protects against all types of malware. According to SoftwareLab.org the five best antivirus products for 2018 are; Bitdefender, Norton, Panda, McAfee and Bull Guard, in that order.

- Do not download any free products from the Internet. Even if you do buy a product on the Internet, check out all the reviews first. Although there is no guarantee that the software you buy will be virus free, always purchase it from a reputable source.

- If you are surfing on the Internet, do not get lured onto sites that do not have a url (universal resource locator), also called the web address, that does not start with https: (Hyper Text Transfer Protocol Secure). The 's' at the end of http means that all communication between your browser and the website you are going to is encrypted. If the site does not have an 's' it is easy for a hacker to intercept your data and read it. Most sites today are secure.

- Before you do business with an online site, that is not a brand name, check all of the references carefully. See how long they go back and what the people bought. If you are not 100% satisfied with what you have read, move on.

3.3 Vishing

Vishing (a concatenation of voice and phishing) refers to phishing over the telephone. While calling someone takes more time and effort, criminals do not have to worry about spam filters. Phone calls are more expensive than email, but Voice over Internet Protocol

(VoIP) services have made mass calling far more accessible to criminals.

These crimes are based on adding value to the data criminals have already purchased on the Dark Web, so they can demand a higher price for it when they resell it. Since they are criminals, they also have been known to sell the same data multiple times. This means that many criminals will have access to the same stolen data. Is it any wonder that we are getting many more fraudulent phone calls and emails?

So what are these criminals phishing for? If they have bought credit card data then they will certainly have card numbers, cardholder names and expiry dates. They might even have the billing address associated with the card. What they probably do not have is the cvv number or the card owner's PIN.

They can easily use a free or inexpensive commercial program to match phone numbers with names and addresses of the stolen cards. A crew might just do this to add more value to the stolen data before reselling it on the Dark Web. They could make a small profit from doing this.

Instead, they might decide to actually phish the cardholder to try and get the cvv number or PIN directly from them. This would make the card data much more valuable.

To do this, they will need to develop a script they can use to lure the cardholder into believing that it is in the cardholder's interest to divulge this information. Some fraudsters are very good at this, others not so much.

If the fraudsters are not good at this, they might purchase a script on the Dark Web and either use it themselves or outsource it to a commercial call centre, like any other business might do. Whatever technique the crew uses, the objective is still the same. Enhance the value of the stolen information by adding new data to what they have all ready acquired.

It is unlikely that they will get new data for all of the stolen cards they have purchased. Even if they only get it for a small portion of the stolen cards, it will make these cards very valuable. The cards that they were unable to get the cvv numbers or cardholders' PINs for will just be resold on the Dark Web, usually at a discount.

Phishing expeditions are almost always carried out on social media or over email. Vishing is only carried out over the phone.

3.3.1 Over the Phone

Some fraudsters will use their crew to contact the target directly. There is evidence to suggest that when a person makes the call, people are more likely to listen and depending on how confident the fraudster is, the target is more likely to turn over their personal data.

These fraudsters usually work out of a boiler room. A plain, nondescript room set up with a desk and chair for each member. The desk will have a phone, a list of targets to call and a script for the fraudster to follow. The background noise and activity in the boiler room will also be conducive to convincing the target that the caller is legitimate.

Not all crews however will have the language skills or confidence to talk to a person, even from a script. These crews might purchase a script from the Dark Web and use a commercial call centre to call the targets. This is more expensive for them, but the response rate is much higher.

Some phone frauds, like the Microsoft computer scam, will also require a specialized skill, like being able to walk a target through the procedure to allow them to connect remotely to their computer. Crews that do not have this skill will almost certainly outsource these calls to a commercial call centre.

Regardless of how criminals do it, there are several common attributes related to every vishing fraud that, if we learn how to recognize them, we can protect ourselves from them. Let's take a look at some of these.

Calls from a blocked or unknown number is an easy way to identify a fraudster. It is extremely likely that they will call from a number you do not recognize, in the hope that you will pick it up. Be particularly wary of calls from outside your area code.

Calls with a three second delay after you pick up the phone is probably coming from a predictive dialler. This is a piece of computer equipment used in a commercial call centre to make the agents more efficient. The predictive dialler places the call from a computer list and waits until the call is answered. If there is no answer, then it moves on to the next call until someone answers the phone. Once the call is answered, the dialler will then route the call to the next available agent. The delay, after the call is answered, and before routing it to a live agent, is usually about three seconds.

Using a computer to play a recorded message is called a robocall. This is a very inexpensive way for fraudsters to try and reel-in a target by telling them something in the message that will make them want to get more information by calling the fraudster back.

Caller id spoofing makes it almost trivial to spoof a caller id number these days. If a scammer wishes to present themselves as an official from say, a government agency, it would be easy for them to show you a legitimate number on your caller id for that agency. Using caller id software allows the fraudster to send or receive outgoing or incoming phone calls or text messages that appear to be from any phone number of their choosing. They might even use your own phone number or a number of a family member.

These are just some of the techniques fraudsters use when vishing.

3.3.2 Protecting Yourself From Vishing
Vishing is not that hard to protect yourself from, if you are using a land line. Yes you heard me right. It really is not that hard. Here are

a few practical things you can do to protect yourself from phishing scams.

- The best way to never become a victim of a telephone fraud is to not answer the phone. Let me repeat that. If you do not talk to the fraudster, you can not be scammed over the telephone.

- The best way to accomplish this is to make sure you have call display and call answer on your phone. When the phone rings, let it go to call answer. Set this feature up so you can hear the caller's message while it is being recorded. You can then decide if you want to talk to them by picking up the phone, calling them back later or not calling them back at all.

A fraudster will probably just hang-up if you do not answer. If it is a robocall, it will probably leave the message. I know how difficult this is to do. When we hear the phone ring, we have to answer it. We are all trained to do this. If you can change this one little thing, it could save you a lot of grief.

There is another big advantage in not answering the phone when it rings. Many of the robocalls we receive are checking to see if a number is even active. Answering will indicate that a person is at this number. Regardless of the outcome of the call, the fraudster already has a good piece of actionable information, that can be resold.

The other risk that you run when answering the phone is that any action you take, may be construed and used against you. For example, if a woman's voice asks if you can hear her, a simple 'YES' might be used later to indicate your agreement to purchase something. The same thing could happen if you are asked to press any keys on the phone during the call.

Cellular phone vishing is much harder to protect yourself from. The Pew Research Centre found in 2017 that 54% of cellular users use public Wi-Fi networks. They also found that over 20% of these users also performed sensitive activities like shopping and banking on their devices. Here are some practical things you can do to protect yourself from phishing scams on your smart device.

- Use a strong password, privacy settings and a fingerprint lock to secure your device and use the auto-lock feature.

- Encrypt the storage and set your device to delete all of the data on it after x number of unsuccessful attempts to log-in.

- Set up a remote wipe of all your data.

- Be able to locate your device if it is lost.

- Set up emergency contact information that is visible from the pin entry screen.

- Shut down Wi-Fi and Bluetooth connections when not in use.

- Public Wi-Fi hotspots are not secure. Use your carriers' network whenever possible or a good quality VPN.

On Tuesday, March 7, 2017 WikiLeaks announced that the CIA had the capability to hack into some smartphones and bypass the encryption software. If the CIA can do it, so can hackers.

- Upgrade your phones operating system and all the apps you have installed as a minimum and keep them updated.

4.0 Major Types of Frauds

It seems like every day, someone wants to tell you about another fraud they have heard about. If you took all of this at face value you would wonder how you could ever make sense of it all.

The bad news is that there are literally thousands of frauds. Just small changes to a fraud can give rise to hundreds of them. They look the same, but they are different in some small way. No wonder people are finding it hard to cope with all of this.

The good news is that there are really only a small number of frauds that are materially different from each other. Yes, there may be thousands of variations of each type of fraud but the underlying motivation for the fraud, the raw emotions they appeal to and the fundamental way in which they are carried out, will be common to all frauds, of a given type.

Once you learn to recognize each major type of fraud, the details of each individual fraud within the type, will no longer matter. In the same way that you may not be able to tell the difference between a California Clapper Rail and a Light-footed Clapper Rail, you can still tell that they are both birds and belong to the same family.

Before we dive into these major types of frauds, I want to explore the basic instincts that we all have as human beings. These are the instincts that drive our behavior. Fraudsters will try to exploit these in each of us to make their scams work.

Human beings have three basic instincts. In no particular order they are;

- self-preservation, the drive to preserve the body, the life and the functions of the body,
- sexual instinct, the drive to extend into the environment and through generations to come and
- social instinct, the drive to get along with other people and form secure social relationships and bonds.

One of these three basic instincts will dominate our reactions and subsequently, our behavior in any given situation. In every person, two of these instincts will be stronger than the third. This creates an instinctual tier structure with a dominant, secondary and tertiary order. The dominant and secondary instincts will always prevail in each individual, with the third one being their blind spot.

All frauds will try to illicit certain basic instincts in the target to try and get them to behave in a particular way that will make the scam successful. We need to learn to use our blind spot instinct to keep us balanced when we find ourselves presented with a scam that appeals to our dominant instinct.

Try to keep this thought in mind as we explore eight major fraud types. We will look at a number of scams in each type, to get a better understanding of how fraudsters appeal to these basic instincts.

4.1 Payment Card Frauds

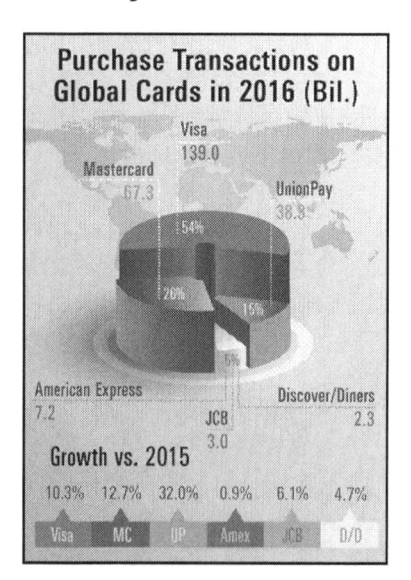

Purchase Transactions on Global Cards in 2016 (Bil.)

Visa 139.0
Mastercard 67.3
UnionPay 38.3
54%
26%
15%
5%
American Express 7.2
JCB 3.0
Discover/Diners 2.3

Growth vs. 2015

Visa	MC	UP	Amex	JCB	D/D
10.3%	12.7%	32.0%	0.9%	6.1%	4.7%

The first major fraud type we want to look at is Payment Card Fraud. A payment card is either a credit or a debit card. Based on the 2018 Nilson Report, there were over 18.1 billion payment cards in circulation worldwide and this number is expected to grow to 23 billion by 2020.

At present, the majority of purchases are made on credit cards. This is changing rapidly however as a result of global demographics, the number of people in underdeveloped countries and the younger generations that prefer to use debit cards. It is estimated that by 2020, 67% of all purchase transactions worldwide will be made on debit cards. For this reason we are starting to see credit and debit cards combined into a single payment card.

The largest increase in payment cards is from UnionPay, an increase of 32%. China UnionPay (CUP) is the only payment card accepted in China. There are already more than 20% UnionPay cards in circulation than VISA and MasterCard combined.

With numbers this large, is there any wonder why payment cards make up the majority of personal frauds? It would not be difficult to imagine that there is anyone who has not experienced a payment card fraud. Most likely, a credit card fraud. This is why I am confident that every credit card number in the world has already been stolen. Here are just a few of the frauds associated with payment cards.

4.1.1 Credit Card Scams

Christopher Thompson, a British furniture seller, introduced the first credit card or at least the idea of buying on credit in 1730. He ran an advertisement in the newspaper offering furniture that could be paid off weekly. This ushered in the idea that people who could not afford big-ticket items could make regular payments until the full cost of the items were paid.

This idea was picked up and used until the early part of the twentieth century by Tallymen, people that sold clothes that the buyers could pay for in small weekly payments. They kept a tally of what people had bought on a wooden stick. One side of the stick was marked with notches to represent the amount of debt and the other side was a record of payments.

In 1914 Western Union gave their more prominent customers a metal card to be used in deferring payments, interest free. This system became known as metal money. Today most people have at least one credit card in their possession. The average person carries four.

Stealing credit card data has become big business. Whether an individual steals your actual credit cards or organized crime goes about it on a massive scale by hacking into your credit card data does not really matter, because the results are the same. The individual is compromised and while credit card companies will usually cover any losses, the victim must still suffer the inconvenience of replacing the card and contacting any vendors that need the information for preauthorized payments. Not to mention the grief they will have if a payment on their card is refused, because the card was cancelled. If you have had to go through this situation, it is not something you will want to repeat.

Since most credit card data is stolen without our knowledge, there is very little that we can do about it. The best that we can hope for is that the security information (cvv number and PIN) related to the credit card has not been compromised. Criminals will be working hard to try and get us to divulge these security codes. They typically use the phishing and pharming techniques that we discussed earlier, to trick us into telling them what they are missing.

Once they have acquired your card's cvv number, here are some of the ways they will use the information.

Card Not Present (CNP)
CNP scams are becoming more frequent as people use the Internet for more purchases. To make an online purchase without showing the merchant the card is easy, as long as you know the card number, name on the card, expiry date and the cvv number.

If the crew has been successful in getting the cvv number from the cardholder by phishing for it, all they have to do is start buying items online. They can store these items and either fence them through another crew or sell them online through an auction site.

Crews that reside in a large geographic area might find it more advantageous to advertise the items themselves using a local classified website like Craigslist. An ad might look like this;

"Samsung 65 inch 4K UHD HDR LED Tizen Smart TV for $600, still in box. Won as a gift, no where to put it. Cash only, on approval. Email CRE245@Yahoo.com for details".

The crew member will already have sourced the item, say from Best Buy, so they know the retail price is over $1,000 for this item, making the sale price very attractive. The email address will only be used this one time. Once the buyer contacts the criminal, they will get the details on where to send the item. The criminal will call Best Buy and order the item using the stolen credit card and cvv number. The item will be shipped to the buyer. The criminal will arrange with the buyer a time to pickup the cash, once the buyer confirms that the item is in good working order. The criminal will collect the cash and return to the crew.

The buyer is happy with their new tv, the credit card owner will see that the item was purchased on their credit card, the credit card provider, when notified of the unauthorized purchase, will remove it from the cardholder's bill and that will be the end of the transaction.

This is happening so often that the police are often never notified. In most cases it is just considered a cost of doing business.

Counterfeiting
A crew that has purchased stolen credit card data without the corresponding PIN information can go to a counterfeiter who will produce a counterfeit credit card that looks and feels just like the real one. It does not matter if they do not have the PIN because most merchants in the country still have not installed PIN readers. These retailers will swipe the credit card and ask the cardholder to sign the receipt to verify the purchase. This is called chip-and-signature verification. Criminals know this and they will only use counterfeit cards at these outlets.

If they are making a large purchase with a counterfeit credit card they may take the extra step and ask the counterfeiter to male up a fake driver's license with the fraudster's picture but the cardholder's name, in case the retailer asks for picture identification.

Counterfeiters buy the stolen credit card information and then using phishing techniques they try to get the cvv number and PIN before producing a counterfeit card. Plastic card printers can cost up to $10,000 but they can produce 6,000 – 7,000 counterfeit cards per day. At this rate, it does not take long to pay for the printer. Credit cards are harder to counterfeit than debit cards because a clerk will usually examine a credit card whereas a debit card is entered into a machine that is only interested in the numbers on the card, not what the card looks like or how the person presenting it might be acting. A clear white debit card works just fine in an ATM.

4.1.2 Debit Card Scams

The public's concern for fraud security is growing more rapidly regarding debit cards than it is for credit cards.

If your credit card data is stolen, the thief still has to sell the information or somehow convert it into cash and typically this can take several steps before the unauthorized purchases are made. Most credit card providers have also limited the liability of the cardholder, so apart from the inconvenience of replacing the card there is minimal financial affect on the cardholder. The average victim of credit card fraud has to spend eight hours and $40 of their own money to combat the affects of a credit card fraud.

While most of us have become sensitized to this inconvenience there are still many people for whom the affect of the fraud is much more significant. For example, anyone with an automatic bill payment on their credit card that has subsequently bounced and affected their credit score or the embarrassment associated with trying to use your credit card when the credit limit has been reached. These situations may not have an immediate economic impact on the victim but it can take the victim a lot longer to recover from these intangible effects.

Nevertheless, this is almost insignificant compared to the affect of debit card fraud on the individual. If your debit card information is stolen then the only thing between you and your cash is your personal identification number (PIN). Although financial institutions generally have better computer security than retailers they can still be hacked.

For some time now, banks have been encouraging people to use their debit cards at retailers, instead of their credit cards. They would like us to think that the debit card is more secure because bank security is better than what most retailers can provide. The other way they are encouraging this is by charging retailers more to process a credit card transaction than a debit card one. This trend is working for the banks and that is why we are seeing estimates that suggested that by 2020 more than two-thirds of all retail purchases will be made with debit cards.

Nevertheless, under federal law your liability for unauthorized use of your debit card depends on how quickly you report the loss. If you report a debit card missing before it's used without your permission, the Electronic Funds Transfer Act (EFTA) says the card issuer cannot hold you responsible for any unauthorized transfers.

If you report the loss within two business days after you realize your card is missing, you will not be responsible for more than $50 for unauthorized use.

However, if you do not report the loss within two business days after you discover the loss, you could lose up to $500 because of an unauthorized transfer. You also risk unlimited loss if you fail to report an unauthorized transfer within 60 days after your bank statement containing unauthorized use is mailed to you. That means you could lose all the money in your bank account and the unused portion of your line of credit taken in overdrafts.

The important thing to remember is that banks are legally allowed up to ten business days to investigate fraud and can freeze cardholders' account access during this time.

With the increase use of debit cards there is also an alarming increase in bankcard frauds in certain parts of the world and this is just a harbinger of what we can expect in North America.

Until merchants start to favor chip-and-pin transactions over chip-and-signature there will not be many debit card scams at the point of sale. Most of these scams will continue to occur at the ATM. Here are just a few of the scams we are seeing taking place at these machines.

Shoulder Surfing occurs when someone looks over your shoulder and watches you enter your PIN. Your PIN by itself is not worth much to a criminal without your physical card. When you end the transaction, the shoulder surfer, who is standing behind you, will distract you, to have you turn away from the machine, while an accomplice grabs your card and runs away. This scam works best on seniors and elderly people.

These other scams all have to do with ATM tampering. This is by far how most debit card scams occur.

The Lebanese Loop refers to a simple piece of plastic that is slightly longer than twice the length of a bank card and is wide enough to cover the card's chip. A fraudster will fold this in half and slide it into the ATM's card reader. Taking the ends that are sticking out, they will place a dab of glue on the inside of each end and fold them back into the reader, so they stick to the top and bottom of the slot. This will allow the debit card to slide through the loop when it is inserted into the card reader. However, it can not be read by the card reader because the chip is covered and it can not be rejected because the tension on the loop is holding it in place.

All the fraudster has to do is take a position from where they can watch the victim enter their PIN and wait. The ATM will continue to ask the victim to enter their PIN, since it can not read the PIN on the card because of the loop. The fraudster will have several opportunities to remember the PIN as the victim continues to enter it. In frustration, the victim will try to end the transaction, but their card is not released because it can not get past the loop.

The fraudster will offer to help and watch the machine while the victim gets help from someone in the branch. As soon as the victim leaves, the fraudster will use a small hooked tool to pull out the loop and the victim's card. They will then head to another branch to clean out the victim's bank account.

Cash Trapping occurs when the fraudster places a plastic cover over the cash slot on an ATM. This cover is an exact match in color and size for the bank machine. This scam works because the top and bottom slots of the cash drawer turn in when it opens and not out. The cash is pushed out thorough the opening. The cash trap fits over this opening and when the cash is pushed out, it gets stopped by the plastic cash trap that has two sided sticking tap on the inside to grab the money. Victims often think that the machine is out of cash and that the transaction has been cancelled. All the fraudster has to do is return later, pull off the cash trap and leave with the money.

Faux Fronts are being placed right over the entire ATM. They fit snuggly on and are a one-piece unit. They are designed to capture all of the data on your card, include whatever you enter through the machine. Think of it as one stop stealing, everything that's on your card is captured. There is very little you can do to detect these state-of-art units from the real machine.

Shimmers are the ultimate debit card theft. It is a small electronic circuit board that fits easily into the ATM's card reader. It takes about 15 seconds to install. The microchip technology is designed to capture the data on your debit card when it is inserted. The fraudster returns later with a small pair of tweezers to remove the shimmer. They can then extract the data, create a blank debit card with the victim's data on it and start emptying their bank accounts.

These same shimmers have also been found in chip-and-PIN card readers to steal people's credit card and PIN data.

4.1.3 Preventing Payment Card Frauds

The most important thing you should know about payment card fraud is that it is getting more expensive for companies. In October, 2016 the Nilson Report confirmed that the cost of credit card fraud worldwide surged to 5.2 cents per $100 of purchases. Previously this had always been below 5 cents. As long as it was below 5 cents, credit card companies accepted fraud as a cost of doing business. They simply wrote it off. This all changed however when the cost went over 5 cents. Writing off the cost is no longer acceptable. So what can we do to help prevent payment card frauds?

Here are some things we should all be doing.

- Speak with your bank or credit card provider and ask if they offer two-step authentication. Different service providers will have their own names for this service. However, they all work basically the same way. When you sign-up, you will get a notification sent to your cell phone, home phone or email with a unique security code whenever an online purchase is made with your card? You then have a short time to enter this code to complete the transaction. Without the code the transaction will be cancelled.

- Check you statement regularly and often. This is still the best thing you can do. I recommend that you go online frequently to do this. The earlier you catch a problem, the better.

- Cover your cvv number. I use a blue dot on mine. You can buy these at the Dollar Store. You might consider the sticky part of a post it note or some painters' tape. Do not double it up or make it too thick since it will have trouble going through a chip reader.

- Cover your PIN completely when you enter it at a terminal. I mean really cover it. Women are much better at doing this than men. Place your hand or wallet over the keypad. Slide your other hand under it and press your PIN. It may take some practice to do this without peaking, but it will be worth it.

- Do not let your credit card out of your sight. Go with it, if you have to. Never let the clerk get between you and your card. It is just too easy to swipe your card twice.

- Use an RFID wallet for all smart cards. Also consider reducing the number of private label cards you carry. Most retailers now take Visa or MasterCard and these providers probably have much better card security than a retailer, like Dillard's or Macy's.

- Use a strong PIN for your debit card and change it regularly. A weak four character PIN is 1111, 2222....9999, 1234, any combination of these four numbers. Over 11% of all PINs used in North America is one of these. Never carry your PIN with your debit card.

- Use a strong and different password for all of your online websites. A strong password is at least 12 characters in length, made up of upper and lower case letters, numbers and special symbols. Try not to use a phrase or English words. Consider keeping a log of passwords and store them in a safe place, away from your computer.

- Never use a private label ATM. Avoid ATMs that are in isolated areas, street corners or parking lots and even in secluded areas of casinos. Anywhere that is out of sight of a camera or security staff. Do not use a debit card at a gas pump.

- As we get older it is always a good idea to go into the branch. Get to know the tellers. They are willing and able to help you, if you need it. Having a stranger in a bank lobby helping you is never a good idea.

4.2 Advance Fee Frauds

After payment card frauds, advance fee frauds are the next major fraud type. There are literally thousands of variations on this scam. The idea is simple enough and very appealing. The fraudster offers you something that you will find attractive. It could be money, a trip, anything you might imagine, but there is only one catch - you have to pay something to get it. Let me repeat that, you have to pay something to get it.

It could be a substantial amount you have to pay if the reward is really big. Would you turn over $2,000 for a chance to get $50 million?

It could be a small amount, only a couple of hundred dollars for the chance to win an all expense paid trip.

It might not involve any money at first, maybe you are asked to do something to help someone and in return they give you a hot tip and tell you about a ground floor opportunity. If you get in early, you can make a killing. All you have to do, is buy in low and sell high.

Some advance fee frauds use the slow drip. They involve very small amounts over a long period of time until the victim has put at risk a large sum of money. The only way to get it back, in their mind, is to continue, until they can cover their losses.

Advance fee frauds appeal to our self-preservation instincts. It triggers the need for financial security. It offers the opportunity to ease one of our major stresses, money.

Here are just a few of the ones we see today. However, there are many other ones and each of these can also have many variations. So do not be surprised if you are presented with one that is slightly different. The thing to remember is, if you are asked to pay anything upfront, then it may be an advance fee fraud. Be vigilant.

4.2.1 Nigerian Letter Scams

According to the Ultrascan Advanced Global Investigations Report, the worldwide losses from this fraud now exceed $82 billion and over one million people have fallen for this scam. It is the most successful fraud in history.

Will Ferguson has written an excellent book detailing this fraud from the viewpoint of everyone involved. "A car tumbles through darkness down a snowy ravine. A woman without a name walks out of a dust storm in sub-Saharan Africa. And in the seething heat of Lagos City, a criminal cartel scours the Internet, looking for victims."

This is an excellent depiction of how compelling this fraud can be and how disastrous the results, to the victim and their family. I strongly recommend that you read it.

The idea behind this fraud is very simple. Someone has died and left a lot of money, usually $50 million or more in an off-shore bank account opened in the name of a person who has the same last name that you have. The account has become dormant and the country's central bank is anxious to close the account and move the money into its reserves.

The local bank manager, where the account resides, has contacted you because you have the same last name as the account holder. He wants you to present yourself as the account holder's relative and claim the money. The bank manager will provide you with all of the background and forms you need to make the claim. He is offering to split the money with you once the funds are released.

There is not much for you to do. You need to prove your identity and fill in the forms. There is no need to travel to the country, the bank manager will take care of everything. You do need to get a FAX machine so the bank manager can fax you forms and the background material you will need.

Everything sounds great so far. You are hooked and can not wait to get the money. However, just before the money will be released, you will get an urgent message from the bank manager saying that something has gone wrong. It does not matter what it is, just something that has come up. Not a problem though, the bank manager can take care of it. You just need to put up $250 so he can make the problem go away. You send him the money and everything is back on track. Right. Wrong.

Every time the money is about to be released, there will be another problem and you will be asked to put up some more money. The longer this goes on, the bigger the amounts you need to put up. If you stick with it, the criminals will even suggest you come to the country to meet with the people involved. This does not end well.

There are over three hundred variations of this one particular letter in circulation. Not to mention the hundreds and perhaps thousands of other types of letters, with equally compelling stories, that are also out there.

4.2.2 Lotteries, Sweepstakes and Prizes Scams

The idea behind these scams are very simple. In each case you will have won something and all you have to do, to claim the prize, is pay a small fee to cover some incidental expense. Usually the fee can be paid by credit card and once you give the fraudster your credit card number, expiry date, cardholder's name and cvv number the prize will be released to you.

These frauds are often carried out over the phone. The criminals who do this are usually very polished. They have done this so often that they sound very convincing. They also have an answer for any question you might raise.

One of these frauds tell the target that they had won a lottery prize. The target thought about this and said they had not bought a ticket for that lottery. The fraudster replied, without missing a beat, that the target's name was drawn randomly from a list of email addresses on the Internet. All the target had to do to claim the prize, was to pay some small local taxes. The fraudster just needed the credit card details and the cvv number of the card being used to pay the taxes and the prize could be released.

Another scam was offering a prize that included a free, all expenses paid cruise for two. When the target was offered the prize they regretted that they were not able to take it. Not a problem, said the fraudster, would you like to give the prize to someone else. The target thought about this and said, yes I would. Can I do this? The fraudster said, of course you can. All they needed was your credit card details and cvv number to pay the port charges, a small amount, and the cruise would be booked in the other couples name. These criminals are very good at what they do.

Everyone wants to be a winner. It's in our nature. These frauds make us feel good. The fees they ask for are very small and reasonable, so a lot of people fall for them.

4.2.3 Travel Scams

Many people purchase airline tickets, hotel rooms, and even entire vacation packages online these days. Scammers know this and there has been a rise in fraudulent travel sites selling fake tickets and non-existent vacations.

Travel is usually a big-ticket item, which spells big bucks for criminals. Additionally, travel is a tricky purchase because you typically pay large amounts of money up front for something that you will not see until the travel date.

According to Webroot, an internet security company, there are, on average, 1.3 million fraudulent websites created on the Internet each month. Most of these only last a short time before being deleted. Some of them are constructed to look like real travel sites in order to dupe unsuspecting people into making bookings on them.

One particularly nasty fraud is related to Airbnb. The fraudsters copy an Airbnb posting of an apartment in a desirable foreign location. Using this information they create an add on Craigslist showing the same apartment but at a discount. When the target contacts them, they are told that the apartment is being offered through Airbnb and they would prefer the target to book it with them directly, for the discounted price, of course.

This way they would be protected under Airbnb's buyers protection plan. So the target would simply make the payment to Airbnb, see the place before checking in and if they did not like it, or it was not as it appeared in the photos, they would get a full refund through the Airbnb platform.

When the target agreed to this, the fraudster send them an email with a link to the property on the Airbnb site. The target made the payment to Airbnb with their credit card and got their confirmation, anxiously awaiting their upcoming vacation.

However, what the target did not know, is that the email sent to them by the fraudster did not have a link to the Airbnb site. It did have a link to fraudster's fake Airbnb site.

This type of scam can be particularly problematic because you may not find out you have been duped until you arrive at your destination or the airport. There may be no record of you having a booking at all. Now you are out the original money and also might have to come up with more to continue on your vacation, or simply pack up and go home.

4.2.4 Continuity Scams

The idea behind a continuity scam is simple. Put a small ongoing charge on the targets credit card in the hope that something small will go unnoticed when the target looks at their statement. The amount is also likely to go unnoticed by anyone looking at the overall total of the bill for some large unusual charge.

The ringtone scam is a particular version of this fraud. Teens and young adults were the primary target for this scam. The fraudsters would advertise customized ringtones on television programs that the target audience watched. You could download a ringtone for $2. What the victim did not notice is that there was a monthly charge for this ringtone.

The fraudsters and the telephone companies all made money from this fraud. In February 2018, AT&T Wireless settled a ringtone fraud by agreeing to pay back $40 million in bogus charges to its customers. It is only a matter of time before the rest of the industry follows.

There are a large range of continuity scams today and they typically follow a similar pattern. Pop-ups for surveys offering free gifts or amazing deals lead victims to enter credit card details to pay for minimal fees or shipping costs. They will also be asked to click their agreement with respect to a long disclosure form with lots of fine print about the survey or related to the gift or the product they just ordered. We have all seen these forms, the print is small, the forms are long and no one reads them. That's the problem.

What we did not read in the fine print is that the fraudster will be billing us each month and the cost of this will be charged to our credit card. The charge might be for another small sample of the cream or pills, that may or may not be delivered to you. The charge might be to help promote the product. It does not matter what it is, but you can expect to be charged monthly for it. The longer you continue to pay without noticing this charge, the harder it will be for you to cancel it.

Typical scams might be related to free samples of creams and pills that have to do with anti-aging, complexion, facial cleansing, diet, hormone therapy and clinical trials. Anything you can think of.

4.2.5 Employment Scams

An employment scam is usually run through email, although it might be conducted within professional networking sites like LinkedIn. These scams are not as common today, with unemployment rates at 3.7%, as they were a few years ago. However, these scams still remain popular with fraudsters, particularly when targeted at older people who could always use a little extra cash.

Working from home has so many draws and is a major lifestyle goal for many people. Fraudsters capitalize on the dreams of these would-be remote workers by luring them with fantastic, yet realistic-sounding work-at-home job opportunities.

You might be asked to become the middleman for transferring funds between people. All you do is cash a check from one person and write another check to someone else, keeping a portion as your fee. Maybe they want you to be a mystery shopper and check the prices of certain items in your local grocery chain. Perhaps your job will have some technical aspect to it and you will need to use a customized piece of equipment or take a course before starting.

The catch? Whatever the job purports to be, the one thing we know for sure, is that the victim will need to send a wire transfer or money order to someone for some seemingly valid reason, before a check that they receive, clears their bank, if it ever does. In short, the victim will be out of pocket by the amount of their wire transfer, without any recourse.

4.2.6 Overpayment Scams

The overpayment scam is very popular on online trading sites and one for sellers to watch out for. It usually relates to the sale of items or services, often through classified ads on Craigslist or on C2C sites, like eBay. The scammer sends you payment for whatever you are selling but sends you too much, called an overpayment. They usually will send you the payment as a check. As soon as you receive the check they will call you and explain that they have made a mistake. They will ask you to refund the difference with a wire transfer or a money order.

The fraudster knows that your wire transfer or money order will clear your account before their check will clear their account, since they have written a check on a fake bank account. So you have received no payment at all, but have issued them a partial refund. The item they bought from you may also have been sent to them.

A variation of this scam is done when the buyer sends the seller a fake pending payment message to encourage the seller to release the item. The fake pending payment message might look like it came from PayPal and the implication is that PayPal has the payment and will pay the seller's account once they receive the tracking information to show that the item has been released. The seller thereby releases the item and the goods are sent. However, no payment is ever received.

Another variation of this scam is that someone sends you check for no apparent reason and you cash it. You may be authorizing the purchase of items or signing up for a loan your did not ask for. So much for consumer protection.

4.2.7 Preventing Advance Fee Frauds

As you can see from all of these advance fee frauds, the over-riding characteristic of all of them is that the fraudster wants you to give them something, usually money, before they give you whatever has been promised.

Here are some simple rules you can follow to never become the victim of an advance fee fraud, no matter how good it sounds.

- Never pay upfront for anything, no matter how good it sounds.

- If something looks too good to be true, it probably is.

- If you know you shouldn't, but you still want to, then take a pause and speak with a good friend. Talk about what is going on and get their advice.

- Do not click on any links sent to you in an email. If you want to go to that site for some reason then put the url yourself into your web browser (e.g. www.airbnb.com).

- Hide pop-ups on your web browser.

- Never click on 'I Agree' on anything you have not thoroughly read and understood.

- Make sure every incoming check has cleared your bank account before issuing a wire transfer or money order to the party sending you the check.

- Never give out personal information to anyone contacting you over the Internet.

- Review your credit card statements regularly for unauthorized charges. Check all items, big and small.

- Before agreeing to anything online, do your own review. Check out any reviews that have been written by others before proceeding.

4.3 Authority Frauds

Authority frauds are also very common. I must get several of these a week. There are innumerable variations of this fraud but the basic idea behind it is always the same. An authority figure is imploring you to contact them about some grave wrong that needs to be corrected immediately.

It might have to do with your bank account, a credit card charge that needs to be confirmed or maybe you have a problem with your tax return. It does not really matter what the crisis is, only that it needs to be dealt with immediately, and only you can fix it.

An authority figure is anyone that the target of this fraud perceives as a person in authority. It does not have to be an obvious authority figure like the police or the government. It might be from a school or church in your area. Maybe it comes from a telephone company or a cable provider, asking about a problem with your subscription.

This is why many authority frauds are done in their names. The email will look like it comes from the bank, the IRS or whatever organization the fraudster purports to be from. It is no longer difficult, to lay an organization's banner over an email header, to make it look and feel like the original.

There may be a good chance that the target does not even use the particular bank, credit card company or computer company that is trying to contact them. Fraudsters know this so they expect a large number of the targets to just ignore them. Nevertheless enough people respond to this kind of exhortation to make it worth the fraudster's while.

Authority frauds appeal to our self-preservation and social instincts. It triggers the need for security and our desire to be part of our society. It offers the opportunity to correct something that is wrong and put us back into harmony with our surroundings. People with strong social instincts usually make good targets for this type of fraud.

4.3.1 IRS Scams

Most people would have no problem believing that the IRS is an authority figure. I do not know many people who would ignore a call from the IRS. Well fraudsters know this and they have no problem pretending to work for the IRS.

These scams are always the same. The IRS has been looking at your returns and there is a problem. It might have something to do with a current or past return. In any case, their examination has indicated that you own them money. How do you want to pay?

Here are just a few variations of this scam and what you might watch out for.

Filing fake tax return scams is a fraud you should be aware of, although you may not even know about it until it is too late. Criminals are stealing our personal information so they can efile a fake tax return in our name. This would be fine if they were gong to pay our taxes, but they are not. Instead they are filing an early fake return designed to get as large a refund as possible without setting off too many flags. The problem is, they are getting the refund. When you go to file your real return the government flags it as a duplicate return and they want to know why you filed two returns. Try to explain that one.

This problem has become so large that if your return gets rejected because of a duplicate filling under your SSN you now have to complete IRS form 14039, Identity Theft Affidavit. This problem is getting smaller, but in 2016 there was $12.2 billion in identity theft tax return fraud. Only $1.68 billion was paid out to fraudsters.

Fake audit scams targets are contacted by someone claiming to be from the IRS or similar tax agency and told that an audit has identified a discrepancy. Immediate payment is demanded with the threat of additional costs, imprisonment, or even deportation if victims do not comply. Whether it is through an email or recorded voicemail, this scam is easy to execute, so it probably will not go away any time soon.

Fake refund scams targets people who are expecting a tax refund. Again, criminals pose as the IRS or similar agency and prompt targets to click a link through which they can claim their refund. However, the link leads to a phishing site where the victim is asked to provide personal information such as their social security number and banking details, which can be used in identity theft.

Erroneous refund scams are a bit more sophisticated as it actually uses real client details stolen from accounting firms via hacking or phishing. The information is used to file a fake tax refund request which is processed by the IRS, and the client receives the refund amount. The scammer then poses as the IRS or a collection agency, tells the client the refund was issued in error, and demands the money be returned. Of course, the payment is directed toward the fraudster, not the IRS. This case spells double trouble for the client. Not only are they short their refund, they could also be in hot water with the IRS for supposedly filing a false claim.

The tax protester scheme is not a scam but bears mentioning. It involves criminals calling or emailing consumers to tell them they do not need to pay taxes. This is really more of a troll than an actual scam, because the person running it does not benefit financially. However, the victim can be negatively impacted, as failing to pay taxes can result in a conviction, including fines and imprisonment.

4.3.2 Credit Card Company Scams

Credit card company scams are often done over the phone. The reality is that our credit card number, expiry date and name of the cardholder has already been stolen. Criminals who buy this stolen data can easily find our phone number. What is missing is the cvv number of the card. Here are some of the scams they use to try and get us to disclose this information.

Potential fraud on your account is used by criminals, working from a script, to try and get us to reveal our cvv number. Here is an actual script that is often used, with some minor variations, to try and trick us into giving up this number. As you read this script ask yourself, if you got this phone call, would you fall for it?

Target: "Hello".
Fraudster: "This is John Peters and I'm calling from the Security and Fraud department at MasterCard. My badge number is 12354. Your card has been flagged for an unusual purchase pattern and I'm calling to verify. This would be on your MasterCard card ending in number 6798. Did you recently purchase an Anti-Telemarketing device for $497.99 from a company based in Arizona?"

Target: "No".
Fraudster: "Then we will be issuing a credit to your account. This is a company we have been watching and the charges range from $297 to $497, just under the $500 purchase pattern that flags most cards. Before your next statement the credit will be sent to you at [insert the victim's home address] is that correct?"

Target: "Yes"
Fraudster: "I will be starting a fraud investigation. If you have any questions you should call the 800 number listed on the back of your card and ask for Security. You will need to refer to this Control Number, 635449. Do you need me to repeat it?"

Target: "No, I've got it".
Fraudster: "I need to verify that you are in possession of the card. Turn the card over. There are 7 numbers, the first four are 6798 the

next 3 are the cvv numbers that verify you are in possession of the card. Please read me the three numbers for confirmation."

Target: "321".
Fraudster: "That is correct. I just needed to verify that the card has not been lost or stolen and you still have the card. Do you have any other questions?"

Victim: "No".
Fraudster: "Don't hesitate to call back if you do."

This is a very compelling story and many people fall for it. However, this is not the only way criminals go about trying to get your credit card cvv number and/or PIN.

The credit card interest rate reduction scams are another one we are seeing. I get several of these a week. You receive a robocall from someone who says you qualify for a program that will help lower your interest rate and pay off your credit card balance sooner. All you have to do is call the number they leave you. This scam is very appealing to anyone who is carrying a credit card balance and paying a 19.9% annual interest rate.

If you do call the number, they will ask you to pay a fee to enrol in the program and the company will work to lower your credit card interest rate. The call may sound like it comes from the credit card issuer and they may even have some of your credit card information, to sound more convincing. They will ask for your cvv number to confirm you have the card and they will charge the service fee to your credit card. What they will not do, is help you to lower your interest rate as promised. You might even be charged if you decline the service.

As you know, not everyone has a chip-and-PIN enabled credit card. Most credit cards in the US are chip-and-signature enabled. As of June, 2017 only 50% of merchants in the country had chip-and-PIN enabled card readers. American Express, Discover and Chase do not even offer a chip-and-PIN enabled card. If you are travelling outside the US, particularly in Canada or Europe, you would be well advised to have a chip-and-PIN enabled credit card. In some locations you might find a card reader that only accepts chip-and-PIN enabled cards.

4.3.3 Bank Scams

Bank scams are usually done over the phone. The pattern is simple and straight forward. You get a robocall from the bank saying that there is a problem with your account. You must call this number, that they give you, immediately to have the problem corrected. You call the number and you get the message we all hate to get, "we are experiencing higher than normal call volumes, please leave your full name, account number and PIN and will get back to you as soon as possible. Thank you for calling [insert name of bank]."

I know, you do not deal with this bank, so you just ignore the call. Nevertheless, many people do deal with this bank and they are worried. This scam hits one of our biggest fears, the loss of our money. The very fact that when you call the number they gave you, all of the lines are busy, increases the panic you feel. You have a strong urge to leave them the information they requested.

Bank vishing scams are some of the most common you will come across. Some criminals might even pose as a financial institution representative and tell you there has been suspected fraud or suspicious activity on your account. They will then try to extract personal or bank account information from you.

4.3.4 Tech Support Scams

These tech support scams, also called the Microsoft scam always follow the same process. Someone will contact you and tell you there is something wrong with your computer. The only way to correct the problem is for the technician to take remote control of your computer. The technician will then do something to your computer. When they have finished, they will probably ask you to pay for the service and ask you for your credit card information.

This scam is not always initiated over the phone and might start via a web page pop-up that tells you that your computer is infected and to call the support number on the screen. The pop-up is usually difficult to get rid of which serves as motivation to call the number provided.

So what did just happen? The first thing that happened is that the technician walked the victim through a series of steps to enable them to take control of the computer. As they did this, they may have pointed out to the victim a number of Windows operating system files and logs to embellish the story that there is something wrong with the computer.

The technician will then download and install a remote access program. They will then do a peer-to-peer link with their own computer, thereby taking control of the victim's computer. They will then download malware to the victim's machine. This might include a keylogger, to track all keystrokes made by the victim, to gain access to their passwords and personal financial data. They will probably install ransomware to get even more money from the victim. Not to mention whatever else they might install on the machine.

Finally, they have all of the information on the victims credit card that was used to pay for the service, including the cvv number. All-in-all, it was a very successful day for the fraudster.

This scam has become so pervasive that Microsoft has begun to take legal action against one of the main companies behind these scams and their affiliates. The civil suit, which has been filed in the federal court of the Central District of California, charges one company with unfair and deceptive business practices and trademark infringement. Microsoft estimates that over 3 million of their customers have been impacted by this scam.

Another version of this scam that we are starting to see is where the scammer pretends to be calling from your bank or financial institution to warn you that your accounts may have been compromised. They explain that they are seeing suspicious activity with regard to a number of accounts and are recommending that you install some protective software on your computer. They tell you it will only take a few minutes and they just need to download it to your computer.

4.3.5 Continuance of Service Scams

Some scammers spend a fair amount of time creating official-looking emails from reputable service providers. They tell the target that the account is about to be suspended and that they need to provide information to keep it going. The email will probably include a link to a phishing site requesting login credentials and billing details to secure the "continuation of service."

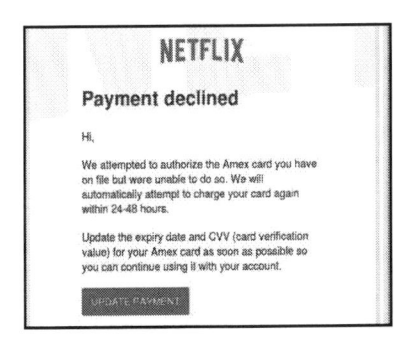

This is a relatively new fraud and the only personal example I have is this one, purported to be from Netflix. The quality of the email is excellent and the graphics are good. It knows that I have paid for Netflix with my American Express card. The red box at the bottom 'Update Payment' is a hyperlink. If I were to press this it would take me to a fraudulent website where it will ask for my card's cvv number. I can assume that they already have my card number, expiry date and cardholder name.

You can expect to get one of these email scams pretending to be from one of any number of common service providers. Anyone to whom you might be paying a monthly service fee. The email will explain that there is something wrong with your account. Perhaps your credit card that is on file has expired, maybe the term of your contract has lapsed or someone has tried to use your account and you need to reset your password. Whatever the reason, it will sound plausible.

4.3.6 Preventing Authority Frauds

There are a number of things we can do to protect ourselves from authority frauds. The most important thing for you to remember is, do not trust what you are told, until it is verified. Here are just some of the things we can do when confronted with someone in authority.

- The very first thing we should do is check it out. Ask the person for a number you can reach them at. Ask them for a badge number or any other personal identification. Offer to call them back after you have confirmed who they are. If they are legitimate, this will not be a problem. If they are not, they will hangup.

- If you are confronted with a robocall, do not panic. Contact the organization the caller purports to represent and ask if there really is a problem, before doing anything else.

- Never click on a hyperlink in an email no matter who the sender says they are. Enter the url in your browser yourself and check it out before getting back to them.

- Go paperless with all of the government agencies, banks and financial organizations you deal with. This will significantly reduce the mail they send to you and eliminate the chance of it being intercepted.

- Continuously monitor your banking and credit card activity online, from a secure location. Never use free WiFi for anything confidential.

- You may qualify for a lower credit card interest rate based on your credit score. If you do qualify, you can get it for free, by simply asking your credit card issuer for a lower rate.

4.4 Rescue Frauds

Rescue frauds appeal to an individual's compassion. The subject of the compassion might be a friend, a family member, a neighbor, a community, victims of a natural disaster, anyone that is suffering a loss or even the individual themselves. Rescue frauds do not have to be about people, they might also be about animals. Saving animals from extinction or providing shelter for them in the harsh winter months.

You have to be particularly vigilant around holidays and any times of pending natural disasters.

These frauds are plentiful in North America and this is not surprising. According to the Charities Aid Foundation (CFA), the US has been named as the world's most generous nation. In 2017 Americans gave $410 billion to charities.

This does not mean that all charities are frauds. Of course not. Fraudsters are very good at inserting themselves among the legitimate charities, hoping to get some of these givings.

These frauds always follow the same pattern. Someone or something that is worthy of the target's compassion, is in urgent need of help. It will always take cash to remedy the situation. The amount is usually not excessive, so the target should have no problem responding quickly to the crisis.

While most of these frauds have a sense of urgency to them, some do not follow this pattern. Romance scams, for example, can take place over several years. Just like a slow drip advance fee fraud, a good romance fraud might also ask for small amounts of money over a long period of time.

Rescue frauds appeal to people who have strong social instincts. They trigger the drive to get along with people and form secure social relationships. These scams offer the opportunity to interact with others to build personal value and achieve accomplishments.

These scams come in many different shapes. Here is just a small sample of some of the ones you might come across.

4.4.1 Family Emergency Scams

This scam is often called the "granny" scam. It is usually targeted at older people. The scam is simple enough. The criminal calls the older person and says, "Hi granny, it's your favourite grandson and I'm in trouble."

They then wait for the older person to say, "Is that you [insert name of grandson]." At this point they acknowledge that they are this person and briefly explain the emergency.

They may have been arrested, perhaps they are hurt, they might have been in an accident, maybe they were robbed, anything that would suggest a sense of embarrassment and urgency. They tell granny not to tell the family, it would be too humiliating. They need cash urgently to pay the hospital, a bail bondsmen, a lawyer or anyone that can help them get out of the situation they are in.

This conversation will never last long. The fraudster will ask granny not to tell his parents or to talk to his family because he is too embarrassed by what happened. He will tell her that she is the only one he can trust to keep this secret and he really needs her help.

After only a few minutes on the phone with granny, the fraudster will pass her off to his accomplice. The criminal is worried that if he stays on the call too long, granny might realize she does not recognize the grandson's voice or the criminal may say something out of character.

The accomplice will now get on the line and explain exactly what granny needs to do and how much money she needs to transfer and to what account, to make the trouble go away. These payments are usually done through a wire transfer or a money order, often through Western Union. The fraudsters do not want granny to have second thoughts and put a stop payment on a check.

4.4.2 Romance Scams

The idea behind a romance scam is not very difficult to understand. Someone decides to go online to look for a companion and a

 relationship that might lead to romance. They might join an online chat group, looking for people with like interests or maybe they join a dating site.

According to Online Dating Magazine, there are over 7,500 online dating sites worldwide. There are over 2,500 in the US alone. Here are just some of the statistics we have for 2018;

- The most popular dating site is Match with over 23.5 million users,
- Over 3 million messages are exchanged on Zoosk a day,
- 49 million people have tried online dating,
- The online dating industry's annual revenue is $1.8 billion,
- Romance scams account for the largest financial losses of all internet crimes.

Fraudsters know that there are lots of targets on these sites. The first thing they do is to start trolling online dating sites, classifieds, chat rooms and social media sites. They are looking for women, age 45 to 65, with money. The ideal person would be someone looking for a long term relationship, trusting, sympathetic and receptive to a sob story. They also need someone that they can convincingly fake a profile to and ideally, someone who will agree to go offline and chat.

This can take a lot of effort, so fraudsters specializing in this scam will usually work in teams. A team might be working multiple scams at the same time. They probably work in shifts and work around the clock. Once they find a target, they start to build a dossier and collect as much information as they can on the woman.

They begin to build a profile of the ideal person for the target. In the cyber world this is called catfishing. They will make sure that they have the right socio-economic background, education, likes and dislikes to be the best possible match for the woman. They will then select a photo to go with the new persona. Not every crew will go to this level of detail, but the more background work they do, the better the scam will be.

So what happens next? Most of these scams follow a similar pattern. It begins with the hook. If the woman is on a dating site, the fraudster will post the ideal profile for her and wait for a match. Otherwise they might make contact in a chat room, through social media or just online using something they have in common to spark a friendship.

The relationship will ramp up quickly with the fraudster being very attentive, sending lots of messages throughout the day over a period of weeks or months. Early in the relationship the fraudster will suggest that they go offline to chat. This is important for the scam because the fraudster does not want the online site to be able to track their chats.

Eventually, after the target has been 'groomed' she is tested. The test might involve a small amount of money. This could be a for a child's birthday gift or to help an elderly relative. At some point the victim may be asked to send something to the fraudster that might compromise the woman later. Maybe a compromising photo or video. Often, the chat history is enough to use as a threat.

In any case, the time will come when the fraudster will threaten the victim to give them more money or to do something illegal. In a surprising number of cases the scam continues for long periods of time simply because the victim is too embarrassed to tell anyone what has happened. In some cases when the victim is not threatened, they know they are being scammed, but want to continue the relationship, so they just keep giving the fraudster money.

4.4.3 Disaster/Relief Scams

It is human nature to want to help people after a disaster strikes. Within hours of a disaster, relief scams start popping up on the Internet. Even before Superstorm Sandy made landfall over 1,000 new websites with "Sandy", "relief" or related keywords in them had been registered, many of these by criminals.

Tragedies inspire people to give. After every disaster there is an outpouring of generosity. Unfortunately many of the people asking for your donations are scammers. They get their word out through spam emails, bogus robocalls and text messages. You find them on Facebook, Twitter and other social media sites. Some even go door-to-door.

These scams follow the same pattern as you would expect to see from legitimate organizations that are trying to help. They will tell you that they are going to provide food, shelter, clothing, medical supplies, transportation to move people out of the affected area, whatever is necessary to solicit your contribution. The only difference is that none of the money they collect, will go to the victims of the disaster.

After Katrina, investigators found over 5,000 questionable Katrina related websites. In their report they stated that the majority of these websites did not provide any aid to the victims. One site AirKatrina.com was set up by a man in Florida who said he was a pilot who was delivering aid to victims but needed help to pay for his fuel. He raised $40,000 in two days. Authorities noted that the site was shut down a few days later.

Many of the websites that criminals set up online during a disaster often have a name similar to well known relief organizations. They might contain a variation of, or misspelling of, Red Cross, Salvation Army, etc..

4.4.4 Recovery Scams

These scams are usually sent to people who have already been scammed three times. Fraudsters know that they can buy a

'Suckers List' on the Dark Web with information on these people, including the scams they have fallen for and the amounts they have lost. They also know that in North America, people who have been scammed once will, on average, be scammed another three times.

Most recovery scams follow the same pattern. The person will be contacted, usually by phone, by a fraudster pretending to be from the police. They will explain that they have been working with international police forces to apprehend a crew of criminals that have been scamming people in the US. They will go on to explain that they have seized their bank accounts and the records of people that have been scammed. They explain that your name was on the list, with a list of the scams you have fallen for and the amount of your loses. They will ask you to confirm this information.

They explain that they are ready to distribute the cash but before they can do this they will need some personal information from you. This information might also include your social security number and bank account information where the money can be deposited.

There are many variations off this scam. Some are done over email, instead of on the phone.

This email explains that the sender is in law enforcement and they have been watching a crew of criminals who are off-shore and are sending out phishing emails. They reference an email you just received.

They go on to say that they know who the scammers are and with your help they want to lure the scammers out so they can catch them in the act. They are able to tell you about other scams you have fallen for and how much money you have lost to these criminals.

They explain that they are working with the local police force, who is on standby to seize the criminals. Once they are in custody they will seize their bank accounts and get back the stolen money. This can then be returned to all of the people they have scammed.

They also explain that you will not be able to get the full amount back, since the fraudsters may have already spent some of it. Although they do believe that they can retrieve most of it, if they act quickly.

All they need you to do, is to pretend to fall for the latest scam, so that they can trace it back to the criminals. This will allow the local authorities to arrest them and seize their bank accounts so they can pay back the people who fell for their scams.

4.4.5 Preventing Rescue Frauds

As you can see from all of these rescue frauds, the over-riding characteristic of all of them is that the fraudster is appealing to your generosity and willingness to help those in need.

Here are some simple rules you can follow to never become the victim of a rescue fraud, no matter how good it sounds.

- Families who want to protect their parents and grandparents from the granny scam should consider setting up a family password that can be used if someone gets this call. All you have to do is ask the caller for the family password. If they do not know it, hang up.

- If you are told to not speak with someone, do the opposite and talk to them. Scams never survive the light of day.

- If you are in an online relationship, tell someone. Do not do this on your own. If you are given a photo, do an image search to find out if you can identify the person. Fraudsters never use their own photo.

- Never put a compromising photo on the Internet. There is no privacy on the Internet.

- Before giving to any disaster/relief fund make sure to check them out and read all reviews before giving. Your preference should be to give to recognized organizations first.

- When you have been scammed three times, no one is going to help you get your money back. Anyone who is duped once should be even more suspicious the next time. Talk with a trusted friend before you give money to anyone.

4.5 Extortion Frauds

Extortion frauds follow the basic premise that you need to hand over money urgently or face a predefined consequence, whether it be real or fabricated. Extortion scams can be simple or extraordinarily complex depending on the imagination of the perpetrator involved. Here are a few of the online extortion scams circulating today.

4.5.1 Ransomware Scams

Ransomware is probably the most common digital extortion scam we see today. It is a type of malware that involves an attacker encrypting your files with the promise of decrypting them only if you pay a fee. It is worth noting that even if you pay the fee, you have no guarantee that the scammer will give you the private key to unlock your files.

One of the most notorious cases of ransomware was the 2017 WannaCry attack in which more than 400,000 machines were infected. Ultimately, criminals took an estimated $140,000 worth of bitcoin in exchange for decrypting users' hijacked files.

Ransomware is simply malware that penetrates computer systems in the same manner that other malware does. You might download it from a fraudulent email link or a flash drive. You might have unknowingly download it after going to a less-than-reputable website.

Like most extortion scams, it works through fear, intimidation, shame and guilt. However the program penetrates your system, ransomware is designed to hide itself by pretending to be something it is not. It might even change file names or paths to make your computer and antivirus software think that it is not a suspicious file at all. The key difference between ransomware and other forms of malware is that the purpose of ransomware extends beyond just mischief or stealthily stealing personal information.

Ransomware acts more like a bull in a china shop. Unlike other malware that is designed around stealth, both before and after invading your system, ransomware designers want you to know the program is there. After the program is installed, it completely takes over your system in such a way that you will be forced to pay attention to it. It has a very different modus operandi than malware designers have traditionally followed. It appears to be the most effective money-making design to date.

Adam Kujawa, Head of Intelligence at Malwarebytes, had this to say, "It's too late once you get infected. Game over." The only options you have are to pay the ransom and hope you get the private key to remove it or do a full system restore from your latest backup, if you have one.

4.5.2 Sextortion Scams

In this form of extortion scam, victims are typically lured into sharing intimate photos or videos. Social media and text messaging might also be the source of the sexual material. They may even be prompted to perform explicit acts while being secretly filmed. They are then asked to pay a fee to prevent the photos, text or videos from being released.

These victims are often found in online relationships through dating sites, social media or chat rooms. Not all online dating sites lead to extortion scams. This usually occurs if the victim is reluctant to send money to the scammer but has already been compromised in some sexual way. It is not uncommon for these relationships to go sour and have the scammer demand money for not posting the sexually explicit material.

4.5.3 Email Extortion Scams

A new and very disturbing extortion scam is making the rounds. The target is sent an email telling them that they have sexually explicit material of the target that will be made public immediately if they do not pay a fee in bitcoin.

The scammer cites a password that the target is currently using or has recently used as proof that they have hacked into their computer. They say that they have taken control of the computer's camera function and have compromising videos of the target. They also claim to have searched the computer's hard drive and have a record of all the sites they have visited. To prevent any humiliation the criminal urges the target to pay a confidentiality fee in bitcoin or the material will be shared with all family members, colleagues and friends.

This can be very scary for some people. However, the cases that have been reported and were investigated indicate that the scammer was not truthful and the target's computer had not been hacked at all. It appears that the passwords were valid, but that they were obtained from previous commercial data breeches. Even though webcams can be hacked, there was no evidence that any actual videos existed.

This scam is different from most of the ones we see because the basis for the scam does not exist. The entire scam has been fabricated. We can expect to see many more of these since they do not require anything more than an active imagination. Here is another one of this type.

4.5.4 Life At Risk Scams

This is another terrifying extortion fraud that follows the same pattern as the last scam. You might receive an email saying that someone has put out a hit on your life. The scammer tells you that they have been hired to kill you, but they are prepared to relinquish their role for a fee. These emails usually contain personal information about you. Certainly where you live and work. They may have pictures of you and your family, even pictures of your home. All of this is intended to make the threat seem more real. They will probably ask you to pay in bitcoin and will include instructions on how to do this. In addition to asking for money, they might also ask you to provide personal information that could be used in a payment card fraud.

There are several other variations of this kind of threat. Some might reference a bomb that has been placed in the building that you live in, or maybe where you work. Most of these emails are only a threat and meant to scare you into paying them. It is very unlikely that you have been targeted.

4.5.5 Preventing Extortion Frauds

Extortion frauds are particularly disconcerting. They can not only be expensive but they can cause a lot of stress on the victim and do a lot of harm to their relationships. Nevertheless there are some simple things you can do to help prevent them from happening to you.

- The most important thing you can do is to never visit potentially fraudulent or risky websites. Most modern web browsers will allow you to filter out unauthorized applications, programs and services from accepting incoming connections. You can do this by turning on your firewall.

- Do not visit sites that look suspicious, especially if you have clicked on a link to go there. Look at the site's url (universal reference locator) to see if it starts with https: (the 's' stands for secure). If there is no 's', only http: do not go there.

- Do not visit sites that are risky. Some web browsers will let you set an alert to indicate if the site you are going to is not a safe site. Heed the alert. Do not visit known risky sites like adult sites. Criminals lurk there, so avoid them at your peril.

- Keep regular backups of your computer. Disk storage has become so cheap that you might even consider doing dynamic backups and recover to the last time anything was saved. You can buy a WD 4Tb (terabit) pocket size drive for less than $100.

- If your computer has been compromised by ransomware, turn it off immediately, disconnect it from the Internet. Do a full system recovering from your latest backup.

- Keep your operating system and software up to date.

- Turn off pop-ups in your browser and be wary of free downloads from music, games and movie sites.

- Disable all webcams when they are not in use. Hackers are able to obtain remote access and record from these devices.

- Use https://haveibeenpwned.com/ to search your email address to confirm possible involvement in a previous hack or breach and change your password frequently if you have.

4.6 Finance Frauds

Very few of the frauds on the Internet are new. Most of them originated a long time ago as telemarketing, direct mail or door-to-door scams. The Internet has added a new dimension to these old frauds enabling the fraudsters to look more professional. A slick website can give the illusion of a large and prosperous company, especially if it has links to creditable, legitimate sites.

The use of email to target potential victims has also allowed many of these frauds to go global at a minimal cost.

Finance frauds become even more attractive in periods of low interest rates, like we are experiencing today. Some pundits are even talking about negative interest rates. It is bad enough to see our investments remain flat, as fund managers eat up any interest our investments might make. Just imagine investing your money and watch it shrink as interest rates go negative.

Under these conditions you can expect finance frauds to flourish. While all of these frauds purport to give exceptionally large returns with almost no risk, this is not the case. The simple economic truth is that the higher the return, the higher the risk. It is like a law of physics, there is no way to get around it. We can all wish it were not so, but this will not change the fact, that it is.

4.6.1 Ponzi Scheme Scams

One of the most successful financial frauds is the Ponzi scheme. When it is executed well, it is very difficult to detect, even for the seasoned investor. This fraud is usually spread by word of mouth. A friend will tell their friends about it and so on.

The scheme is named after Charles Ponzi, who carried out a large fraud of this type in the 1920s. This scam is not new and has been around at least since the 1840s. It was referred to by Charles Dickens in his 1844 novel, The Life and Adventures of Martin Chuzzlewit.

The scam itself is simple enough. A very wealthy and successful investor with impeccable credentials, is willing to invite a select group of people to invest with them, with the promise of significant, short-term returns. The investors can withdraw their initial investment at any time and leave. Does this sound too good to be true. Well it is.

Here is how it works. The victim turns an amount of cash over to the fraudster. In this example, let us assume it is $10,000. The amounts can be any size, but the larger the amounts and the more people who participate in the scheme, the longer it will last. It becomes a virus that feeds on itself as more people find out about it and want to participate.

The fraudster has promised everyone a large return. In this example, say 10% every quarter. Every three months you will get a check and you can take your initial investment out at anytime.

Suppose ten people participate initially. The fraudster has collected $100,000. After the first three months, he gives each of them $1,000, for a total of $10,000, as a return on their initial investment. After a full year, he has returned to them $40,000. Of course there is no investment and he is giving them back some of their own money. At the end of the first year, he still has $60,000 of their original money.

Nevertheless, the investors are delighted. Each of them start to tell their friends about the scheme and they also want to invest. In a very short time the fraudster is collecting a lot of money.

Some of the investors may want their original money back, but this is not a problem, because he is collecting more money from new investors than he knows what to do with. Many of the investors who got in early may have already been paid out more than their initial investment, so most of them just leave their money in. Why not, they have already made a profit. As long as enough new investors continue to put money into the plan, everything is going along just fine for the fraudster.

However, in all of these schemes, the time will come when there are no new investors and the fraudster, who has spent much of the money collected to support a lavish life style, can no long make the quarterly payments. The scheme goes bust and everyone remaining in it, loses their money.

As attractive as these schemes appear, we have to remember that if something sounds too good to be true, then it probably is.

4.6.2 Pump & Dump Scams

Pump and dump scams are highly illegal. They refer to a situation where a small group of informed people buy a stock before they recommend it to thousands of investors. The result is a quick spike in stock price followed by an equally fast downfall. The perpetrators who bought the stock early sell off when the price peaks at a huge profit.

Most pump and dump scams recommend companies that are traded on the over-the-counter bulletin board (OTCBB) and have a small number of shares available for public trading. These are often called micro-cap stocks.

Small companies are more volatile and are easier to manipulate when there is little or no information available about the company.

There is also a variation of this scam called the short and distort. Instead of spreading positive news, fraudsters use a smear campaign and attempt to drive the stock price down. Profit is then made by short selling the stock.

To show how easy it is to carry out this scam, we need only look at Jonathan Lebed. In September, 1999 Jonathan, who lived with his parents in Cedar Grove, New Jersey was about to start high school. He talked his parents into buying him a computer. In the summer of 1999 he had earned about $500 from odd jobs. He asked his father if he would open an over-the-counter trading account for him so he could invest the money he had earned. He was not old enough to do this for himself. His father opened the account and Jonathan started high school.

During his freshman year, Jonathan opened over 150 false email accounts that he used in chat rooms to promote the eleven penny stocks he bought. He also told teachers and friends at school about these good deals. Within six months he had made over $750,000 by promoting these stocks, pumping the price up and then selling them.

In February, 2000 the SEC had noticed this unusual activity and they called on Jonathan's father, who owned the accounts. It soon became clear to the investigators that the father knew noting about this. That's when the SEC realized that Jonathan, a minor, was to blame. This created a problem for the SEC since they did not want to publicize the fact that this pump and dump was perpetrated by a minor. They were worried that it might encourage other minors to do this.

So they settled out of court with Jonathan, who paid a $250,000 fine without admitting any wrongdoing. Jonathan got to keep almost half a million dollars.

4.6.3 Debt Consolidation Scams

These scams are targeted at people who have accumulated a large amount of debt and are having difficulties getting out from under it. Fraudsters use robocalls, email and the Internet to reach these people. They have well designed and attractive websites to lure people in. Make no mistake, there are a number of legitimate companies that will help you to consolidate your debt, but you have to sift through the fraudulent ones to find them.

Tom's story is not uncommon. He was targeted by a debt consolidation scam in which a telemarketer offered a service to reduce his debt by 50% or more. Here is his story.

"I was contacted by a company, and was asked if I needed help with my debt situation. I was interested in what they could do and they explained that they could lower my debt by at least half if I qualified.

The caller asked for a lot of my personal information, including my Social Security Number, credit and banking information so he could analyze my situation. He indicated that I qualified and that they could lower my debt from more than $25,000 to approximately $11,500 if I signed up.

The company said that with all my information, they would negotiate a lower rate from my bank and lower my monthly payments. The fee was almost $3,000, but it seemed like a good deal considering how much it would reduce my debt.

They took the fee from my bank account but, after a couple months, nothing else had happened. When I asked my bank about it, they said they had never been in contact with the company.

When I called the company back, they told me they were negotiating with the bank and everything was fine. That did not make any sense, so I asked for proof. They transferred my call and then hung up on me. When I called back, they became hostile.

I contacted my bank to open a new account so that the company could not access any more of my money. I wish I had done some research on the company and checked with my bank before agreeing to the service and providing my personal, credit and banking information."

4.6.4 High Yielding Investment Scams

These scams, often called a HYIP (high yielding investment program), play on the victims desire to get a better rate of return on their investments without incurring any additional risk. Fraudsters who specialize in these scams often have some experience in the financial markets. They sound like they know what they are talking about. Many of these scams originate in Europe and have now been opened up to Americans though the Internet.

I just did a Boolean search on "HYIP" and found almost 4 million hits on Google. Many of these were websites that promise you a very high return on your investment.

Two of the most common approaches involve offshore investing and access to prime bank instruments that are high quality and low risk.

Offshore investing scams might sound attractive at first but they need to be carefully scrutinized. Some very smart fraudsters have invented some impressive sounding, but meaningless terms, to explain the huge rates of return you can get from these offshore markets. Just remember, return of your money is much more important than, return on your money.

Beware of investments using any of these terms;

• Pure or common law trusts,

- Prime bank guarantees,
- Standby letters of credit,
- Underwriter liabilities or
- Bank debenture programs.

Every one of these terms are absolutely meaningless. Everyone is made up. They might sound good but they are all fake.

Prime Bank scams is another common type of HYIP sold by fraudsters. There is actually a thread of truth to these. That is what makes them so attractive. The term 'Prime Bank' does refer to the fifty or so largest banks in the world and they do trade in extremely large investments, but this is where the similarity ends.

The fraudsters often tell their potential investors, that they have special access to programs that otherwise would be reserved for top financiers from the world's financial centers. Doesn't that sound good. They might go on to say, that these programs involve trading in international financial instruments and that profits of 100% or more are available with little or no risk.

Here are just a few of the instruments that they might mention to you;

- World paper,
- International monetary fund (IMF) bonds,
- Prime bank guarantees,
- Medium term notes or
- Prime bank debentures.

You should be very wary when you hear these terms or some variation of them. Fraudsters looking to lend legitimacy to their cause often use these terms. However, neither these instruments nor the markets on which they allegedly trade, exist. That's right, none of these are legitimate financial instruments and there are no markets in which they are traded.

Regardless of the type of HYIP scam the fraudster choses, there are several characteristics that are common to all of them.

The fraudster will maintain that all transactions must remain private and confidential. They will assert that bank and regulatory officials would deny the existence of these instruments and you may be asked to sign a nondisclosure agreement. References will also not be available because of the extreme secrecy.

The fraudster will claim that this opportunity is by invitation only and that only a handful of very exclusive investors will be allowed to participate. They might even suggest that historically these opportunities have been reserved for the wealthy elite.

The fraudster will guarantee enormous returns, maybe 100% or 200% a month without any risk to your principal.

The fraudster will also be very vague about who is involved in the transaction and where the money is going. They will often explain that these instruments are too technical or complex for non-experts to understand.

In most of these cases the money raised from investors is just spent by the fraudsters. They will manufacture financial statements to show that the money is being invested to buy these bogus instruments and after a time they will simply tell the investors that they have lost everything. They will say that market conditions caused the collapse and there was nothing they could do.

4.6.5 Preventing Finance Frauds

These scams can have a devastating result on the victims. In many cases these frauds are perpetrated on seniors and elderly people because fraudsters know that most of them have a nest egg so they target them.

Here are some practical things we can do to help protect us and our loved ones from these frauds.

- If you have an older relative that might be a target of one of these scams, talk to them and explain how these frauds work. Encourage them to call you if they are ever presented with one of these 'opportunities'. When light is shed on a fraud it usually gets exposed before any damage is done.

- The other thing to remember is, if it sounds too good, then it probably is. You should not expect to get a return that is much higher than the average of what the markets are giving.

- The best thing you can do when presented with any opportunity is to not act quickly. Sleep on it and make sure you speak with a trusted friend or advisor. A fraudster will try to pressure you into acting quickly. They know that if you think about it and talk to someone about the opportunity you will not act. Most frauds never survive a thorough due diligence.

- Think before you invest in anything. Perform your own due diligence or get a trusted advisor to do this for you. Verify the identity of the people involved, the veracity of the deal and the existence of the security in which you plan to invest.

4.7 Elder Frauds

While many types of internet frauds can target virtually anyone with access to a computer, many are crafted specifically with the elderly in mind. Seniors are often targeted for frauds since they are perceived as being more susceptible to certain scams. The truth is quite different. They are a very homogeneous group and therefore it is easier for fraudsters to pitch to them, than say, millennials, who are not as homogeneous.

Fraudsters know that seniors all have similar interests. They are concerned about their finances, no one wants to outlive their money. They are concerned about their health, the high cost of health care and their quality of life. They are also very concerned about their family. This is why so many of the frauds aimed at this group have to do with these issues.

Here are some of the more common frauds targeted at seniors and elderly people.

4.7.1 Investment Scams

Seniors know that their money has to last them. They do not know how long they will live, so any investments that seniors make need to be secure. They can not risk losing their principal because they probably do not have the time to replace it. However, they also need a reasonable return on their investments or their quality of life could be affected. Fraudsters also know this.

Investments scams to the elderly will often be through the mail, on the phone or via email. Fraudsters working these scams are themselves often older people. They know how to sound professional and they can even make the flimsiest idea sound like a sure thing. These fraudsters know that the appearance of professionalism combined with polite manners or overtures of friendship may often lead many older people to accept their advice.

The other way fraudsters promote themselves is through investment seminars. These seminars are promoted by promising motivational speakers, investment experts, or self-made millionaires who will give you expert advice on investing. They are designed to convince you into following high risk investment strategies such as borrowing large sums of money to buy property or investments that involve lending them money without security or on other risky terms.

Promoters make money by charging you an attendance fee, selling overpriced reports or books, and by selling investments and property without letting you get independent advice. The investments they offer are generally overvalued and you may end up having to pay fees and commissions that the promoters did not tell you about.

High pressure sales tactics or false and misleading claims are often used to pressure you into investing, such as guaranteed rent or discounts for buying off the plan. If you invest with them, there is a high risk that you will lose your money.

4.7.2 Insurance Scams

The insurance scam plays on the assumption that seniors might be less focused on what they have now and more so on what they will leave behind for loved ones.

This type of scam might involve a letter or pamphlet being sent to the senior, advertising the purchase of a paid-up insurance policy that guarantees the face value of the policy plus any interest earned over the life of the policy. The fraudster will follow up with a phone call and a meeting with the senior to discuss the details and how the policy works.

The scammer will have promotional material with them on how the policy works and answer any questions the senior may have. They will also be able to go online to the company website so the senior can see how substantial the company is and how prosperous the business. They will ask the senior for the one-time premium on the policy. They will sign the policy and the copy, then ask the senior to sign both the original and copy. As they leave, they will remind the senior to store the policy in a safe place.

What the senior does not know is that the website they were shown was an excellent fraud. The company does not exist and the paid-up policy they just bought is worthless.

These fraudulent websites never last for long. They will be deleted within a few weeks or maybe a month and the same website will spring up with a different name.

4.7.3 Health Scams

As people age, health tends to be more likely to deteriorate and the need for prescription medication can become expensive. Many online pharmacies have stepped in to offer drugs and other healthcare at lower than average prices. The problem is, most of these sites do not operate within the law or follow standard practices. For example, the founder of Canada Drugs is wanted in the USA for selling counterfeit medicines, but the website is still very much up and running. Without proper regulation, consumers really have no way of knowing what they are getting or if they will receive anything at all.

4.7.4 Preventing Elder Frauds

These frauds can have a devastating affect on elderly people. There is the obvious affect of losing their money, that in its self, could be crippling. There is also the impact It could have on their self-esteem and the impact it might have on their family. No one wants to be duped. Everyone thinks that they can take care of themselves, but as you get older, you worry more about these things.

If you are a senior or elderly person, here are some practical things that you can do, to prevent yourself from becoming a victim of one of these frauds.

- If you are presented with any financial opportunity after a certain age, slow down, take a deep breath and talk to a trusted friend, a relative or a financial advisor about the opportunity. Do not make this decision on your own and never act hastily.

- Get guidance and direction from a legal representative on putting in place a Power of Attorney (POA) before you need it. Too many people wait until it is too late.

- The person holding your POA becomes an excellent resource for you to speak with if any financial opportunities do arise.

- Choose someone else, a relative, a lawyer, an accountant or your banker who can ask for a regular accounting from your POA to ensure that your best interests are being looked after.

- Do not be afraid to revoke your POA if you have any concerns.

4.8 Identity Theft/Fraud

Identity theft and identity fraud are two terms we hear a lot about today. So what do they really mean? Identity theft is defined as the unauthorized access to personal information. It can occur without identity fraud, such as through data breeches. Once the theft is used for illicit financial gain, it is then considered identity fraud.

It is estimated that in 2018 Identity Fraud increased by 8%, rising to 16.7 million people and victims lost $16.8 billion. Fraudsters are getting more sophisticated in their attacks, using stealthier and more complex scams.

In most studies Identity Fraud is broken into the three categories, originally defined by the FTC (Federal Trade Commission).

• Existing card accounts, including credit and debit cards.

• Existing non-card accounts, including checking and savings accounts, existing loans, insurance, telephone and utility accounts.

• New accounts and other account frauds.

For our purpose, we are not going to deal with the first category, existing card accounts, since this has already been addressed in the section on payment card frauds.

Let's start with Identity Theft.

4.8.1 Identity Theft

As we already said, Identity Theft is not Identity Fraud. I know that the press likes to lump these two things together. Whenever you read about a major computer breech, the press will often call this Identity Fraud.

The truth is that Identity Fraud is a targeted crime. It is directed at a specific individual for a specific reason. If a computer hacker steals the data on a million credit cards or 164 million email addresses from LinkedIn, as they did in May, 2016, they do not care who these numbers belong to. They are just a set of numbers that they can sell over the Dark Web.

This does not mean that criminals may not be interested in obtaining personal information on you. The more information that fraudsters have on you, the more valuable the information is, when it is resold on the Dark Web. Criminals who do not have the skill to hack into a computer system, might use one of these methods to obtain your personal information.

Stealing your purse or wallet is a very low tech way to get more information on you than your payment card. Wallets, not so much, but a purse is a treasure trove for a fraudster. Every woman I know carries too much in her purse. It is not uncommon to have several credit cards, a stack of loyalty cards, a bank card, a driver's license, a health insurance card, a list of your prescriptions or medications and maybe a bill you might be carrying in your purse for payment at the bank or even a check book. You might even be carrying your social security number. Did I leave anything out?

Stealing your mail is also popular with criminals, especially if you have a community mail box instead of home delivery. Criminals have been known to steal cluster box units or even the larger neighborhood delivery collection box units. They might slip a chain around the bottom of the box and pull it free with a pickup truck, then throw it in the back and drive off.

Both of these methods are random. The fraudster has no other reason to steal your personal information than they can. In all likelihood they will sell this information on the Dark Web and it may or may not be used in an Identity Fraud. In most cases it will probably result in a payment card fraud or a cashed check and nothing more serious than this. However, if a fraudster does decide to target you, here are few other things they might do to get a more thorough picture of you, before attempting a more serious Identity Fraud.

Breaking into your house is also a possibility if the criminal has already targeted you. It is unlikely that a fraudster would do this randomly. However, if you live in an upscale area and you drive a flashy new car and wear expensive jewelry, then they might decide to break into your home, to see what personal information you may have there. This is a bit extreme but for very complex identity frauds this does happen.

Steal or sifting through your garbage is another way a fraudster might find out more personal information about you.

Check your credit score by posing as your landlord, employer, recruiter, or any other person authorized to access your credit report.

Bribing employees of companies you are associated with; where you work, bank, get your health care or anyone who might have your personal information in their files. This is a very common practice.

So what do the fraudsters do when they have stolen sufficient information to successfully impersonate the victim? How do they turn this into an Identity Fraud?

4.8.2 Existing Non-Card Account Scams

The second category, existing non-card accounts, is usually perpetrated by someone the victim knows and the amounts are usually relatively small compared to the other two categories.

An example of this type of fraud would be when the victim writes a check to pay for something. The person receiving the check then covers their name, the date and the signature and puts the check through a bleach bath. A container filled with a specific mixture of bleach and water through which the fraudster slowly moves the check back and forth until the amount of the check has been removed. The check is then dried and the fraudster writes in a new higher amount and cashes the check. In many cases the higher amount might go undetected, especially if the victim is a senior or someone unlikely to regularly balance their check book.

A much more common example of this type of fraud occurs when someone gives a trusted friend or relative control over their finances. We often see people doing this to try to avoid probate fees or estate taxes. An elderly parent might give a child joint custody of a safety deposit box, right of joint survivorship to an investment account or a Power of Attorney (POA) over their financial affairs. Whatever the original intentions of the two parties at the outset of the transaction it is very hard to predict how this arrangement will end up.

4.8.3 New Account Scams

The third category, new accounts, is the one I do want to spend some time on because these are by far the most damaging for the victim. These frauds do not happen to many people, but when they do, they are responsible for almost half of the total amount stolen in identity fraud. This type of fraud is also harder to detect.

As a rule, the more complicated the identity fraud, the more costly and the more time consuming it will be to correct the damage caused by the fraud. The good news however is that most criminals are opportunists and they are always looking for the easy score. They would rather do a credit card fraud than perpetrate a more complex identity fraud even though the rewards of the later are much larger. They would also prefer to carry out a simple identity fraud instead of a more complex one.

As unsettling as it is to have a fraudster run up credit card charges in your name or make withdrawals from your bank accounts it is more devastating when they open new accounts in your name and use these accounts to perpetrate other frauds.

An accomplished fraudster can obtain a counterfeit driver's license, credit cards and even open bank accounts and investment accounts in your name with nothing more than your social security number. Your SSN is probably the most important piece of identification you have.

Home equity loan frauds are harder to do today than they were before the housing bubble burst, but they are still a favorite of many identity fraudsters. This is how they work.

The fraudster will usually cruise an area and look for a home owned by a senior. The senior might be out doing some gardening. They will stop and introduce themselves as a realtor working in the area. They will ask the senior if they would be interested in selling their house. The fraudster can usually get the senior to give them all the information they need to perpetrate the fraud by asking prying questions about the value of the home, whether the owner still has a mortgage on it and if so with whom and for how much. Most fraudsters would prefer to find a home that is owned free and clear.

Once the fraudster has selected a home to target they might intercept the homeowner's mail to get the rest of the identity information they need. This would include bank statements, credit card bills and anything with their social security number. A sophisticated fraudster would not keep the mail, just open it to get the data they need, reseal it and put it back into the homeowner's mailbox. They do not want the homeowner to know that the mail has gone missing.

With this information they can begin assuming the owner's identity. They can get a counterfeit driver's license, with the fraudster's picture on it, counterfeit credit cards, with the fraudster's signature on it, and counterfeit social security card made up. They can also open a bank account in the victim's name but with the fraudster's signature.

They can then apply for a home equity loan on the victim's property. Once the loan is granted and the money put into the fraudster's bank account, the fraudster and the money disappear.

It does not take long for the lending organization to realize that the loan is in arrears and come looking for the homeowner.

4.8.4 Other Account Scams

In extreme identity frauds the criminals will sell the home out from under the victim.

To do this they will target two victims, a homeowner and a second victim that an accomplice will impersonate as a straw buyer. In the case of the homeowner they will continue in a similar way as described above. In the case of the straw buyer they will not need to pry information from them but might just intercept their mail to get the data necessary to counterfeit their driver's license, credit cards and social security card.

When they have stolen enough data from the two victims and opened bank accounts in their names they are then ready to execute the fraud.

They will execute a sale by owner to avoid needing a realtor for the transaction. The fraudster's accomplice (straw buyer) posing as the home buyer will apply for a mortgage with a bank or other financial institution. The two fraudsters will each engage a lawyer to complete the paperwork and once the deal is closed and the funds distributed, the fraudster, posing as the home owner, will split the mortgage amount with the fraudster, posing as the home buyer, and they will both disappear with the money.

After an identity has been stolen in this type of fraud, the time and effort it will take to clean up the mess can be considerable and costly. It is estimated that it might cost the victim as much as $1,000 in legal fees and it could take years to correct the problem.

4.8.5 Preventing Identity Theft/Fraud

While the number of these frauds are very small, the size of the damages can be very large. Very few people will actually be a victim of Identity Fraud, but in order for one to be perpetrated on you, the fraudster needs to assume your identity. The best way for you to prevent this from happening is to develop a few good habits with respect to protecting your identity, in the first place.

Here are few practical suggestions that you can follow to make sure your identity is protected.

- Lock your social security number in a safety deposit box and only take it out when you really need it. If you do not have a safety deposit box, then hide or lock it up in your house. Do not carry it with you. If you have copies of important papers at home with your SSN on them, use an indelible marker to redact the number.

- When you go out, only carry what you need. If you are a woman, learn to live without a purse.

- Buy a good quality in-home shredder. One that has a cross-cut, not a strip cut, these are two easy to put back together. A cross-cut leaves the paper looking like confetti. Use it before throwing out any documents with your personal information on it.

- If you have personal and confidential documents at home, buy a lockable filling cabinet to store them in and lock it when you are not at home. Do not worry about the quality of the cabinet, you only need to know that someone has tampered with it to alert you to an intrusion.

- Put a strong password on your home computer. Keep it locked and turn it off when you are not using it.

- Install a good home security system. If your home is well protected, criminals might just move on to another target where it is easier to get at their personal information.

- If you still write checks, buy a gel pen. These are inexpensive and are widely available. A gel pen uses a pigment that is suspend in water-based gel that can not be erased, even in a bleach bath.

- If you have home mail delivery, consider putting a lock on your mailbox. Better still, signup for electronic delivery of all important mail and stop paper delivery of anything that has personal information on it.

- Get regular credit reports. A federal law allows consumers to order one free credit report annually from each of the three credit bureaus. Stagger your requests so you get one credit report every four months. Check for any credit card or loan accounts that you do not recognize.

- If you suspect that you have been the victim of identity theft ask the credit reporting agencies to put an alert on your account. This requires that lenders contact you before extending credit. Even though they are supposed to work together it would still be worth your while to contact each of them separately. Depending on the credit bureau, the alert might expire in ninety days, so you may need to reactivate the alert periodically.

Although it is difficult to protect yourself from identity fraud entirely, fraud alerts are a strong first line of defence. By working with the credit bureaus and taking a proactive stance your credit report is more likely to be shielded from identity fraudsters.

If you suspect that you might be the target of an identity fraud against your home or other property you own, consider securing a lien against the property. This is the easiest way to thwart an identity fraudster who might try to sell your property without your knowledge. A lien can be as easy as having a line of credit, a small loan, taxes owing or any other encumbrance against the property. Fraudsters will always take the easy path and look for property that does not have a lien against it.

5.0 When You Become a Victim

The probability that you have been or will be the victim of a fraud is very high and increasing every day. It is very important that you be prepared when this happens and you know what action to take to minimize your risk.

If you think you have been tricked into giving out your credit card, debit card, PIN or bank account information to anyone, then follow the instructions below.

1. Contact the card issuer or bank quickly and report what has happened.

2. If necessary, cancel your card or bank account and open a new one. The bank or card issuer will advise you on what to do.

3. Review your billing or banking statements carefully and report any unauthorized transactions immediately. If the item has not been reversed on the next statement or bill, send a letter (or FAX) to the card issuer describing each questionable item.

4. Change the PIN on all your cards immediately. People often have the same PIN on all their cards so it is easier to remember. If one has been compromised change all the others.

In the United States
If you believe your personal identification information (social security number, etc.) has been compromised or stolen and you might therefore be the victim of identity fraud, then follow these instructions.

1. Immediately contact one of the three major credit reporting agencies and explain the situation, Equifax (1-800-525-6285), Experian (1-888-397-3742) and TransUnion Corporation (1-800-680-7289). Whichever one you contact, they will notify the other two.

a. Request that they place a fraud alert and a victim's statement in your file. You will receive a confirmation in the mail that a fraud alert has been placed with all three agencies.

b. Request a copy of your credit report to check whether any accounts were opened without your consent.

c. Request that the agency remove inquiries and or fraudulent accounts stemming from the theft.

2. Contact your bank(s) and ask them to flag your accounts and to contact you regarding any unusual activity. It is always best to do this in person.

   a. Close any bank accounts that were set up without your consent.

   b. Get a new bankcard, account number and PIN.

3. Contact your local police department to file a criminal report. Ask for the case reference number and the officer's name and telephone number. If you obtain a copy of the police report make sure it states your name and SSN.

4. Contact the Social Security Administration's Fraud Hotline (1-800-772-1213) to report the unauthorized use of your personal information. This is an automated telephone service. They do not publish the phone numbers of local offices. If you are hard of hearing the TTY number is 1-800-325-0778). You can speak with a Social Security representative between 7:00 am and 7:00 pm Monday through Friday. You will generally have a shorter wait time if you call during the week after Tuesday.

5. Notify your local Department of Motor Vehicles (DMV) to report the theft and check to see if an unauthorized license number has been issued in your name.

6. Notify your local Passport Office and report the theft. Ask them to watch out for anyone ordering a passport in your name.

7. The Financial Crisis Inquiry Commission (FCIC) has put out an excellent little booklet called "ID Theft: When Bad Things Happen To Your Good Name". You should request this online. It is available as a pdf document. It is free and easy to download.

8. Keep a diary of the names and phone numbers of everyone you speak to regarding the incident. Document any follow-up phone calls with letters and copies of all correspondence.

In Canada
If you believe your personal identification information (social insurance number, etc.) has been compromised or stolen and you might therefore be the victim of identity fraud, then follow these instructions.

1. Immediately contact one of the two major credit reporting agencies and explain the situation, Equifax Canada (1-800-465-7166) or TransUnion Canada (1-866-525-0262 or 1-877-713-3393 in Quebec). Whichever one you contact, they will notify the other one.

   a. Request that they place a fraud alert and a victim's statement in your file. You will receive a confirmation in the mail that a fraud alert has been placed with both agencies.

   b. Request a copy of your credit report to check whether any accounts were opened without your consent.

   c. Request that the agency remove inquiries and or fraudulent accounts stemming from the theft.

2. Contact your bank(s) and ask them to flag your accounts and to contact you regarding any unusual activity. It is always best to do this in person.

a. Close any bank accounts that were set up without your consent.

b. Get a new bankcard, account number and PIN.

3. Contact your local police department to file a criminal report. Ask for the case reference number and the officer's name and telephone number. If you obtain a copy of the police report make sure it states your name and SIN.

4. Contact the Canadian Anti-Fraud Call Centre (1-888-495-8501) to file a complaint and to report the unauthorized use of your personal information.

5. Notify your local Department of Motor Vehicles (DMV) to report the theft and check to see if an unauthorized license number has been issued in your name.

6. Notify Passport Canada and report the theft. Ask them to watch out for anyone ordering a passport in your name.

7. Keep a diary of the names and phone numbers of everyone you speak to regarding the incident. Document any follow-up phone calls with letters and copies of all correspondence.

6.0 Summary

Personal fraud is something that is becoming so invasive in our lives that it is almost impossible to find anyone who has not been a victim. Fraud is becoming so insidious in our life that it is almost impossible to escape.

The very best we can hope for is that the next time we come across fraud that we will recognize it for what it is and that we will know how to respond.

It can still seem quite daunting when you look back on what you have read and try to decide what you need to do to protect yourself. Not everything you have read may apply to your particular situation. I get it. So what do you really need to do. Everything that came before were suggestions to reduce your risk of being a fraud victim. Here are the five recommendations that you really need to act on immediately.

- **Protect your online and mobile devices** with a screen lock, finger print access and use strong passwords, at least twelve characters in length, with a mixture of upper and lower case letters, numbers and special characters. Encrypt data stored on these devices. Avoid public Wi-Fi and use a VPN. Install antivirus software and keep it up-to-date. With us relying more on our digital devices to obtain goods and services, making purchases and sharing personal information, fraudsters have shifted their focus to these devices for the access they can provide to accounts and the information they store or transmit.

- **Protect yourself from unauthorized online transactions.** As chip-and-PIN makes fraud at physical stores more challenging, criminals are now targeting online merchants. Some financial institutions even offer advanced alerts for online transactions, for example, Verified by Visa and SecureCode by MasterCard are just two you can sign-up for. These can help quickly detect and even prevent online fraud before it happens.

- **Use two-step authentication wherever possible.** Enabling two-step authentication on sites that have that capability, where a separate action must be taken beyond providing a username and password to access an account, can make it significantly more difficult for fraudsters to take over your accounts. Check with your service providers to see if they offer this feature.

- **Sign up for account alerts everywhere.** In addition to placing an alert on your credit report, a growing variety of organizations including credit card issuers, brokerage firms, email and social media providers offer customers the option to receive notifications of suspicious activity. These notifications can often be received through email or text message, making some notifications immediate, and some go so far as to allow their customers to specify the scenarios under which they want to be notified, so as to reduce false alarms. Check with all of your major service providers to see what they can offer.

- **Place a freeze** on your credit report to prevent anyone else from opening one in your name. This is especially important if you have been a victim of a data breach that has exposed sensitive personal information. There is a small charge for this and the freezes must be placed with all three credit bureaus to prevent everyone, except existing creditors and government agencies, from accessing your credit report.

7.0 Closing Remarks

I would like to thank you for buying *Fraud Awareness*. I hope you enjoyed reading it as much as I enjoyed writing it.

Personal fraud is not going away, it is just getting more pervasive. I hope the suggestions in the book will be of value to you. I hope that the description of the major fraud types will make it easier for you to recognize a fraud, the next time one is presented to you. But more than anything, I hope you will share this book with others who might benefit from Fraud Awareness.

In particular, please share it with a senior or elderly person, since they are the primary target for fraudsters today. They are also the most vulnerable. They will benefit the most from the book.

I am often reminded of president Ronald Reagan's comment about the Soviet Union, a major threat during his time in office, when he said of them, "trust, but verify". One of the biggest threats to us in the 21st century is going to be fraud. Perhaps the phrase we should be mindful of is, "do not trust until verified".

If you enjoyed the book and it was helpful to you, please take a few moments to write a review on Amazon. Reviews are important to an author because in many cases they are the only feedback we get. Reviews can also be invaluable to others, like you, who are just looking to find some practical ways to protect themselves in this very complex world.

Mike

8.0 About the Author

M. J. Veaudry holds a Bachelor Degree in Computer Science and an MBA. He has held a number of senior management positions in  the computer industry and was a partner with one of the world's largest professional services firms. As a management consultant, he has worked in the USA, Canada, South America, Europe and Asia.

As a computer industry executive Mike became interested in the prevention of computer fraud. This has led to a lifelong interest in understanding how frauds are perpetrated with particular focus on personal fraud. As a policing volunteer, he offers community programs on Fraud Prevention. He is also the author of *Fraud: Don't Be A Victim.*

As a gaming aficionado, he has had a lifelong interest in playing and betting strategies as they relate to Las Vegas table games and slot machines. He has written two books on gambling, *Mike's Guide to Better Slot Play* (#1 Best Seller on Amazon) and *Casino Games Demystified.*

Mike has been visiting Las Vegas since 1984 and he has been a property owner here since 1994. *Las Vegas Travel Tips*, updated annually, is a compilation of the best things to do and see in Las Vegas when you are not in a casino.

Mike and his wife travel extensively and they love to cruise. *Ocean Cruise Travel Tips*, updated annually, is Mike's second travel book. It is based on a passion for cruising and the combined years of experiences of his and his friends at sea.

Mike is currently working on his next travel book, *Hawaii Travel Tips*, to be released next year.

Other Books by M. J. Veaudry

If you enjoyed this book, you might also enjoy some of the other books by MJ Veaudry that are available on Amazon in both paperback and eBook format.

Fraud: Don't Be A Victim

Fraud: Don't Be A Victim takes a look at fraud in six common venues; credit cards, debit cards, telephones, email/internet, identity theft and street frauds. These are the areas where fraudsters are likely to try and scam us.

In each of these areas we will explore the kinds of frauds that are common today and how fraudsters try to dupe us.

We will then discuss a number of practical ways to protect ourselves.

All frauds have several common characteristics. Once you learn these you will be better able to recognize a fraud and take the steps necessary to ensure you do not become a victim.

The book will also tell you what to do if you do become a victim of fraud and how to minimize your exposure.

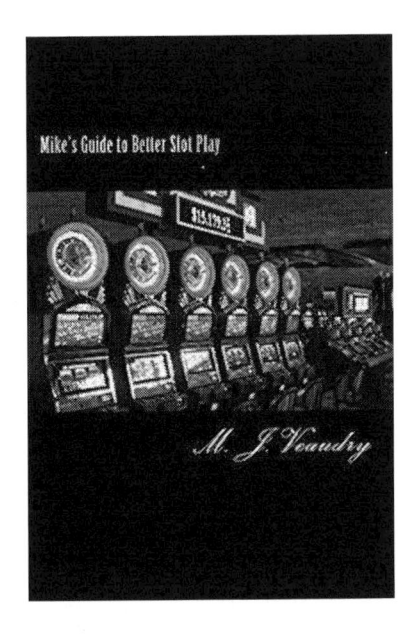

Mike's Guide to Better Slot Play is the best selling book on playing slot machines on Amazon. It has over 80 reviews and a 4.5 star rating.

Mike will explain how slot machines work. He will take you through a simulation of a machine to show what is actually happening inside.

Using this information he will show you a process with rules, techniques and strategies to improve your slot play. A proven way to manage your money better so you can leave the casino with more of your winnings.

Casino Games Demystified will explain the fundamentals of six popular casino table games; Three Card Poker, Roulette, Let It Ride, Pai Gow Poker, Blackjack and Craps.

Learn table etiquette, the rules of play, a sound betting strategy and step-by-step instructions on how to get to the table and play with confidence.

There is even a list of free online sites where you can go to practice before hitting the tables.

Las Vegas Travel Tips is full of personal reflections on things to do and see when you are not gambling in a casino. The book is based on Mike's thirty years experience in Las Vegas.

The book covers planning ideas before the trip, information on finding discounts, the best shopping, the best spas and several outstanding tours that will bring you up close and personal with the wonder and beauty of the Mojave Desert.

There are chapters on entertainment, the author's pick of the must see attractions and of course, dinning out.

Ocean Cruise Travel Tips covers selecting a destination, choosing the right cruise line for you based on price/performance, brand, passenger demographics, amenities and loyalty programs.

The book is loaded with personal experiences and full of tips to get the most out of your next cruise.

The book also has lots of references to websites that will save you time planning your next cruise. It will tell you how to get alerts when prices drop and where to get the best deals.

Hawaii Travel Tips, Mike's next travel book is expected to be released in 2019.

Made in the USA
Columbia, SC
10 March 2019